On Becoming Toddlerwise

Books in this Series

ON BECOMING

TODDLER

WISE

*From First Steps
to Potty Training*

GARY EZZO, M.A. AND
ROBERT BUCKNAM, M.D.

ON BECOMING TODDLERWISE
From First Steps to Potty Training
Published by Parent-Wise Solutions, Inc.

© 2003 by Gary Ezzo and Robert Bucknam, M.D.
International Standard Book Number: 0-9714532-2-5

Cover Photo:
Photographer Eric Tucker
Getty Images, Inc.

For information:
Parent-Wise Solutions, Inc.
2130 Cheswick Lane, Mt. Pleasant, SC 29466

03 04 05 06 07 – 10 9 8 7 6 5 4 3 2 1

Dedicated To:

Ashley
First to call us Grammy and Grandpa

ACKNOWLEDGMENT

Acknowledgment of indebtedness is made to the host of contributors for whom this book would not have been possible. Leading the pack are our faithful editors including the amazing wit and style of Diane Wiggins. Joining Diane is Tiana Wendelburg and Kendall Woods. We note a special thanks to Carla and Joey Link of J & C Ministries for their organizational talents, friendship and contributions to this work, specifically authoring Chapter Five, 'Structuring Your Child's Day' and portions of Chapter Nine, the 'Toddler Topic Pool'. Stephanie Taylor graciously brought her expertise to Chapter Seven, 'Potty Training Made Easy'. She was joined by Deirdre Salmon and Jenice Hoffman. Other contributors include Susan St. Clair, Pam Stanley, Luona Nightingale, Shannon Herring, Julie Young, Dana Ott, Carol Mohr, Pamela S. Ramont, Cyndi Bird, Tracy Burner, Roni Hathaway, Anne Ratliff, Jocelyn Schumacher, Jeana Owens, Karen Kurtz, Karen Forden and last but never least, Anne Marie Ezzo.

CONTENTS

CONTENTS

INTRODUCTION

Let's face it. There is no end to a toddler's creative expression, from munching on crayons to striking a Superman pose while standing—oh yes—on the grocery cart seat when your head is turned to the artichoke bin. A toddler's day covers a gamut of challenges, including small tantrums in the pizza shop because there is a bubble on the cheese to tantrums at naptime because he is just too tired to rationalize the benefits of sleep. But there is a tender side of the same child.

Watching a wide-eyed toddler smile as Mom gently blows the tuft of silky white hair of spring's last dandelion into the air, and then seeing a spontaneous clap of little hands, bears witness to the amazing reservoir of joy this child brings. A toddler takes his mother's hand and pulls her toward the toy box because he remembers the pleasure of yesterday's play and wants to share the moment with Mom. When little hands pull a face close to touch noses or plant a kiss, a world of turmoil comes under the spell of a toddler's expressions of love. All is at peace. The power of a toddler's embrace, the joy of his smile, the comfort of his cuddling, all teach us about a simple love that is pure and unmeasured.

As educators, parents, and grandparents, we know of no greater fulfillment that a parent can receive than the upturned face of a child, eyes speaking wonders and a face of confidence in discovering the world with you. This is what makes parenting the most interesting subject in the world. In just over a year, the helpless infant emerges as a little moving, talking, walking, exploratory person marked by keen senses, clear memory, quick perceptions, and unlimited energy. He emerges into a period of life known affectionately as the Toddler Years.

On Becoming Toddlerwise concerns itself with this brief but significant window of growth, this vibrant period of your child's life, from taking his first steps to mastering toilet training. The second year of life is an amazing, spontaneous, engaging yet challenging time for the emergent child and his parents.

In view of the fact that a toddler's mind is driven by curiosity, a need to investigate and a tendency to try and rule the world with a smile or a scream, it becomes essential to consider the influence of the home as the principal learning environment, and Mom and Dad as the principal teachers. The self-evident truth that early family life lays the foundation for later adjustments exists above all other assumptions.

As to the technical side of this book, it was our decision to use the masculine references of "he," "his," and "him" in most cases. The principles of this book will of course work just as well with raising daughters. Also, because the toddler phase does not follow chronological age, you will find some references to 14-to-40 months. This reference represents the broader period of toddler concerns even though most of this book is directed toward the second year of life, 12-to-24 months. Finally, we do not claim nor insist that this is all the information you will need to raise a toddler; it would take volumes more knowledge than we possess. Therefore, parents guided by their own convictions have the ultimate responsibility to research parenting philosophies available today and make an informed decision as to what is best for the family.

Thank you for letting us share in your unique adventure in parenting.

Gary Ezzo, M.A.
Robert Bucknam, M.D.

Chapter One

What's Inside The Package

*N*ature has a keen way of tutoring parents. Observe the gardener with his plants. He does not create the bloom, or the petal, or the stem that produces the petal. He cannot grow the plant or make it more beautiful. He is neither its creator nor its architect. The power of life and beauty lies within the plant itself. The gardener however, knows the environment. He knows the right amount of sunshine and moisture required for the unfolding of every blossom. He knows the time of pruning, training, and fertilizing that is necessary to bring the plant to a beautiful bloom. Yet the gardener is neither the life of the plant nor the source, but he is the nurturer of the life placed before him.

Picture your toddler's life unfolding like a beautiful bloom. You, the parent, serve as the bloom's keeper. No other influence can affect the life of your child quite like you—a loving, caring parent. You are more than a nurturer of nature; you are the guardian. You matter greatly in the life-formation of your child. This leads us to observe the real work of parents as loving mentors.

We know that toddlers are not merely men or women of smaller stature. They are not miniature adults either physically or mentally.

The emerging toddler has his own peculiar way. He thinks in the here and now, with no tomorrow in sight. He is not easily moved to self-restraint or control to secure some future blessings. "A penny saved is a penny earned" is quite beyond his grasp and interest. And all his peers would agree that crying over spilled milk is essential if you're really thirsty—you'll get more milk faster that way!

Your toddler will first be concerned with the concrete, not the abstract. Moral qualities such as justice, mercy, and truth are quite beyond his reach, but he does understand these qualities when expressed toward him. His actions and developing speech reflect his self-oriented desires rather than socialized values that will change in a few years.

Clearly the adult life, while distinct from childhood and adolescence, is wholly built upon the foundation of the early training parents put into their children. It is important to see that a child is adequately prepared from the beginning for a safe arrival in the many stations of life, starting with understanding the little person emerging under your roof.

What goes into making a toddler indeed a person? There are a variety of influences, including things you cannot control (nature, heredity, temperament, and predispositions), and those influences shaped by your beliefs (nurture, environment, education, values, and goals). There is also the natural order of growth and development of the species, which brings new and changing variables into play. As the child's body grows, so grows his mind, and so grows his interplay with the rest of humanity. All these factors together make up the human quality of our being. Let's talk about nature, starting with the timeless subject of heredity.

A Toddler's Life is Controlled by HEP

Little Joey swings a stick and suddenly he's slated for College All-Stars twenty years down the road. Abby twists a silk scarf around her neck and suddenly she's destined to be a fashion designer following her momma's footsteps. Far-fetched? Not exactly. We are all influenced by the forces of heredity, environment, and personality. Nineteenth century Dartmouth College professor, H. H. Horne in his book *Idealism in Education*, links these relationships in plain words:

"Heredity bestows capacity,
Environment provides opportunity, and
Personality recognizes capacity and improves opportunity."

Each force combines together to shape all of us—you, me, your sweetheart napping in the next room. The same Professor Horne is credited with saying, "A child is born in part, he is made in part, and in part he makes himself." Heredity, it has been said, determines what we can do, and environment determines what we will do. Supervising all three aspects are the caretakers of life—enter stage right, Mom and Dad.

Heredity

After conception, nothing can be done to add to or subtract from our hereditary endowment. If Grandpa's left ear turns out along the back edge, just like your mother's left ear which looks amazingly like your own, guess what? Don't be surprised if one or more of your beautiful blooms sports the telltale Grandpa ear. Other traits, while not vis-

13

ible to the eye, are doled out with equal clarity. Is there a trait in your toddler that you do not like? Take a look at the family photos hanging in the hallway. The relative who's smirking is possibly to blame.

A child inherits one-half of his genetic self from his two parents, one fourth of his characteristics from the four grandparents, and one-eight of his biological distinctiveness from eight great-grandparents. Heredity passes to each generation two categories of traits—fixed and fluid. Fixed genetic traits are immune to nurturing influences. Fluid tendencies however, are greatly impacted by the nurturing process.

For example, outward distinctions such as red hair, green eyes, short arms, big ears, cute nose, and dimpled chins are fixed endowments. They are what they are, straight from the genetic cabbage patch. Have you ever wondered where that nose came from? Nothing in genetic sight among the parents? "Your baby got that from Uncle Fabio, on your mother's side," says Aunt Regina. A hidden surprise from the family tree.

Heredity also passes fluid endowments. These are propensities, tendencies, and capacities. Intelligence potential, aptitudes and special levels of giftedness are all fluid, meaning this side of the hereditary equation is markedly influenced by the nurturing environment. That is why heredity determines what a child can do, and the environment determines what a child will do.

Our friends Dave and Suzanne are talented musicians. They each play a combination of instruments including harp, piano, trumpet, guitar, flute, trombone, French horn, and the snake- charming oboe. Their children, Jill and Steven did not inherit their parents knowledge of music, but they did inherit from them an ear, aptitude, capacity and interest in music. Natural propensities spawned in the right environment produced, in this case, multitalented, musical children.

But the genetic endowment was nurtured. Without the nurturing environment, the beautiful seeds of endowment, like the frozen pods in the tundra, lie dormant until the conditions are right to bloom. Unfortunately, human environments are less predictable than seasonal ones.

What does this mean for you and your toddler? If the nurturing environment is to stimulate genetic potentials, and maximize those potentials, it needs three things from Mom and Dad.

First, you need awareness. Gary Ezzo's father was a talented musician. He played a number of string instruments and the piano with pep. One of Gary's brothers inherited this musical talent; two did not. When the Ezzos were raising their children they knew there was a possibility for some musical giftedness. But possibility does not equate to certainty, and it was soon realized that no great musical genetic endowment fell on their offspring.

The point here is that of awareness. The Ezzos knew of a genetic propensity for musical ability. Because of it, they created a nurturing environment to determine if any gene slipped through the family line, and then responded to the opportunity by introducing formalized music lessons in their children's primary years.

What is in your family tree? Go back two generations, to parents and grandparents, and write up a list of endowment possibilities. Talk to relatives, great aunts and uncles, and older cousins. Was Grandpa highly inventive? Was Mom an artisan of quilts? Was there an uncle gifted in mathematics, or a sister endowed with a massive vocabulary and a creative mind? Become aware of the genetic endowments of your recent family lineage. Maybe you'll find a squirrel in your family tree, which will finally account for Billy's need to store up every scrap of paper, every piece of ribbon, and every pebble he ever touched.

Second, you can maximize your child's genetic potential when you parent the "whole child" rather than just a single trait. Hurray for you if your child is a budding Rembrandt, Mozart, Galileo or Edison, but can he entertain himself when playing by himself? Can he get along with other children? Can your little star kick a ball and gently spend time with baby sister? Don't err like Schroeder's mom did. Schroeder is the *Peanuts* character that spent his entire cartoon life hunched over a piano composing music.

While any unfavorable parent attitude can result in unhealthy outcomes, that which has the most damaging and far-reaching effect is the concept of the dream child. Parents create a genetic ideal and force the child into a very narrow category of interest. As a result, the emotional pressure to attain dream child status, mixed with the lack of normal childhood experiences, hinders genetic potential if not wounds it.

Third, no wonderful gift of hereditary endowment can be matured if not surrounded by the basic disciplines of life. Writing the latest, greatest American novel will be impossible if your would-be author never develops the focus needed for reading. Piano practice becomes a battle if your child never learned to sit and concentrate in the toddler years. NBA star Michael Jordan didn't make it to the top of his field simply because of ability; he also learned to listen to the instruction of his mentors along the way. Listening is half of the educational process. How well does your toddler listen to your instructions and follow through—right now?

The point here is basic: a child cannot learn until he is ready to learn. He cannot achieve until the biological clock says it time. He cannot master any skill without the accompanying resources of self-control and self-governance. This means that regardless of what giftedness or talent your child possesses, or what wonderful genetic endowment he may have inherited, it needs to be nurtured in the total context of childhood and childhood training. If it is not, that giftedness, while possibly discovered, will eventually reach a plateau in learning and show little improvement from that time forward. Remember the gardener analogy? Good seeds planted in poor soil will result in stunted plants. So it is with our children.

Environment

With both heredity and environment, children are recipients. Regarding the environment, the home has the dominant control. Mom and Dad provide the environment for the most impressionable years of life. The difficulty, if not the downfall of *laissez-faire* parenting is not realizing how education shapes the habits of the heart, and in so doing weds genetic propensities with right stimulation. The positive forces of heredity do not always find a healthy and nourishing environment. When good capacity is denied the right environment, the legacy is at best less than a child's full potential, and at worst a generational disaster.

What can a reader glean from this fact? One supreme thought— the decisions you make today, the beliefs that drive your decisions, and the parenting assumptions you hold dear can and will affect generations to come.

Personality

Energetic Noah does everything big. He'll march into a room, all smiles, and give Grandma a great big hug. Hopping to the room's center, he delights his eager audience with an impromptu performance. Finally, in grand finale, he drops to the floor to roll himself out the door. When Mom calls him to sit beside her, he cries, and staying true to the end, his distress and resistance is huge. Is his high-flying, crash-and-burn style a sign of a testy temperament, or are we now in the personality zone? What's the difference anyway?

Let's take a look. Few words used in contemporary theory of child development are as ambiguous as the term "personality." The term suggests a variety of meanings to different investigators. We have all heard the expression, "he's a chip off the old block," implying that personality is inherited and not subject to change. Not so on both accounts.

We provide a very simple definition for the sake of continuity. Personality is a composite of three variables: heredity, environment, and temperament. Temperament (inborn into human personality) speaks to the general categories of uniqueness, which greatly influence a child's perceptions and reactions. You can distinguish between a child's temperament and his personality by saying that temperament traits are inborn while personality traits are the result of nature and nurture.

Heredity is what your genetic history brings to personality, environment is what the home and society add, and temperament is the child's contribution.

If that sounds confusing then take relief with this bit of news. Your child's personality is the last thing you need to worry about.

That's because personality is the sum of each influence pressuring the formation of our being. It is not one definite, specific attribute; rather it is the quality of the individual's total behavior. You cannot change the whole without changing the parts, and some parts cannot be changed.

For example, you cannot change your child's temperament anymore than a leopard can change its spots. You can understand it and cooperate with it, but not alter it. You cannot alter the hereditary influences on your children, but you can minimize the negative propensities, strengthen areas of weakness, encourage areas of strength, and maximize areas of giftedness.

The only area you have enormous influence over in the formation of personality is in creating the right educational environment for your children. Education impacts personality. The intelligence environment fostered will make all the difference in the world for your toddler.

When we speak of education we do so in the broadest sense. This goes way beyond textbook learning. Learning and schooling are not synonymous, but both are vehicles of education. Most of your parenting will be devoted to educating your children in three vital areas of life until they achieve mastery themselves: morality, health and safety, and life skills.

Your child's personality is greatly shaped by your educational fervency. You will teach your child to be kind, good, caring, patient, generous, and responsible. You will also help him form healthy habits—how to brush his teeth, take a bath, and manage his personal care. Accenting these educational goals is more education, teaching the child how to think, make sound judgments, and apply logic and reason to his life.

The next chapter continues our discussion of the factors of learning by looking at influences that are neither hereditary nor learned, but part of a toddler's unfolding development. What happens to the mobile toddler?

Chapter Two

The Walking, Talking, Curious Toddler

His little legs can carry him where his curious mind will take him, and his hands touch what his mind directs. One of the most rapid areas of your toddler's development is that of control over different muscles of his body. This developmental achievement is significant and signals a new milestone. Unlike the newborn that cannot move himself from where he has been laid or grasp a toy that was handed to him, your toddler moves with freedom of desire. Mobility multiplies a toddler's ability to learn a thousand-fold.

Throughout the toddler years, two processes dominate: growth and learning. These processes are interdependent, but not interchangeable. Growth refers to the biological changes and maturation taking place in his physical development; learning pertains to the mental processes, which include moral training and development of life skills. Achieved in your toddler's second year is one of the most important milestones of life—your toddler's ability to walk. This growth skill emerges around the same time that the mental process of curiosity ripens.

Put mobility and curiosity together and you have the essence of toddlerhood. The old adage "strike while the iron is hot" has developmental implications for this season of life. Curiosity plus mobility puts a child in the center of a critical phase of learning, where knowledge and habits produce life-long consequences. The toddler years are the learning fields and mobility multiplies the opportunities and certainly creates new challenges for parents.

The Walking Milestone

Your toddler's mobility is nothing new. First he covered ground by creeping, then crawling, standing and then moving from object to object and one day it happened—he took that first step. From that point forward, his world changed and so did Mom and Dads. Walking is a developmental milestone because it marks a new era of toddler independence. Now his little feet can take him where his mind desires. Since the child is on the go, it also means Mom and Dad are not far behind. So a mobile toddler ushers in a new era of parental supervision.

Walking increases a child's contacts. Mobility opens doors of opportunity and new areas of interest, exploration, and adventure. He is also able to walk to mischief and trouble. As a crawler you knew his range of exploration. As a walker, you now must keep your eye on him since his ability and resolve to get from here to there far exceeds his judgment of caution and safety.

During the one-year span between 12 an 24 months, the walking, talking, exploring toddler multiplies the demands of mother's time, energy and patience more than any other period of his life. It is also a time when clashes of the will abound, for the walking-about toddler is in the process of not only testing his legs but also trying new experiences with his hands. His mind has also caught up with his legs, so asserting himself accompanies his mobility. If left to himself, unhindered by moral and safety concerns, this little person can empty a book shelf in minutes, connect with Hong Kong on Dad's cell phone, drink from the bird-bath, splash little hands in the toilet, drain the last sips of leftover beverages, flee the kitchen with a table knife, or take a nap in the dog house—which, after all else, would be a positive thing.

Ah yes, the mobile toddler. There is no question that a toddler's mom is a tired mom, and for good reason. The emotional and physical energy needed to supervise an energy-packed tot can take down the most physically fit mom. If your toddler happens to be a boy, add fifty percent more energy. Never so beautiful does this child look to his weary mom as he does when he closes his eyes in sleep.

Thus, walking is one of the great milestones of life. It is the single most important skill that unlocks a brand new world waiting to be discovered. While his little legs will propel his body, there is another process going on inside that propels his mind. It is the natural endowment of *curiosity*.

Curiosity is a Toddler's Delight

Seasoned moms know that a little mud, whether on your toddler or in his stomach, won't really ruin his dinner, and to the curious toddler, a bowl on the head makes a great space helmet even if it is filled with pancake batter. Is curiosity an impulse or drive? We do not know, but a toddler has a reservoir of it, and for good reason.

Whether endowed by creation or nature, curiosity is a mechanism of the brain, serving as a stimulus to learning. There are two types of stimuli, *direct* and *natural*. A parent sitting with a book reading a story to an attentive two-year-old is an example of a *direct* stimuli. Are direct stimuli important in the chain of knowledge? Absolutely! However, curiosity is a *natural* stimulus—a child's birthright—a survival mechanism. It is the key that unlocks the treasures of toddler knowledge and opens a world of discovery. Curiosity is a corollary mechanism of logic and reason.

Curiosity is also the precursor to your child's developing imagination. Curiosity drives the child to investigate and explore items of interest, to touch and handle, to walk away only to revisit it again. Between the ages of two and three, curiosity becomes less dominant and imagination begins to take over. The natural endowment of imagination is a function of play as much as it is a function of learning.

For example, RJ only showed curious interest in the Tommy Train box cars and engine received on his second birthday. He touched the tracks, he spun the wheels, and even tried to stack the cars. But he did not understand the play purpose of a train. But at three years-of-age, curiosity gave way to RJ's developing imagination. Now a more dominate cognitive process begins to rule RJ's thinking. At three he plays the role of engineer. His mind constructed mountainous terrains out of pillows, wobbly bridges from a shoe box top and special tunnels through legs of chairs. Train sounds began accompanying each circle of the track as the train became real in RJ's mind. Big changes took place in one year. The same will happen with your toddler.

At three years of age, make-believe and other imaginative activities begin to occupy an important place in the child's mental world. Imagination will do what curiosity cannot. It will carry a child beyond the boundaries of time and space. Through imaginative processes a child gives life to inanimate objects, while assuming a controlling role as chief operator of his own play.

In our next book, *On Becoming Preschoolwise*, we investigate the significance of a three-year-old's imagination, and how it propels the learning experience beyond curiosity. We will explore the influences that turn the imagination on and what can delay its maturity. We mention this here only to highlight the fact that while curiosity will play a dominant role in the early days of your toddler's expanding world, it is only a precursor to another very important mental process yet to unfold, the development of your child's working imagination.

A child's curiosity is almost unlimited. He is interested in everything, including himself. Yet curiosity is not an end unto itself, nor is it profitable without parental supervision. The duty of a parent is to neither deny nor suppress their toddler's curiosity, but to manage it. We will say right up front that giving a toddler unlimited freedom to go along with his curiosity is not useful management but rather poor stewardship of a child's mind.

What do we know about curiosity and children? First, curiosity is but the first piece in the educational process of discovery. Associated with curiosity are the activities of attention and investigation. All three are necessary components of learning for young toddlers. Consider the first step.

Curiosity

For toddlers, everything in their unfolding world is new, exciting and worthy minimally of a glance. It is the newness of an object or activity that provokes toddler interest. Winding the grandfather clock with Dad, making funny faces in the mirror, watching a cord get plugged into an outlet, or hearing a blow dryer and feeling the warm air on his hand, all fall under the spell of curiosity. Understand that curiosity itself is not the teacher of your child rather it is the impulse or vehicle that takes him to the classroom environment of potential learning.

Potential is the qualifying word. The essential characteristic of a stimulus that arouses a toddler's curiosity is its novelty. Toddlers explore novel objects and then turn to other things when the novelty dissipates. A matter as simple as opening and closing a door, or turning a faucet on and off satisfies these moments of curiosity and becomes a source of enjoyment as long as the activity remains novel and slightly challenging. When turning the faucet on and off becomes too easy, it is then abandoned. The novelty wears off, but the memory of discovery stays intact.

Use this fact to your advantage. Those nasty touching habits that trouble a mother's clean soul—a child's hands in the dog dish, his preoccupation with the toilet seat or the trash can are new and novel attractions. How should you manage these unhealthy and potentially dangerous challenges? Help the child lose interest in them, not through suppression or distraction, but by substitution.

To *suppress* is to deny the child a specific action. To *distract* is an attempt to redirect the child to a new activity. *Substitution*, in contrast, offers an equally desirable experience similar to the original one that caught your toddler's curiosity, but the place and timing will be under Mom's control.

For example, that little splashy hand in the dog's water dish produces amusement and laughter for your thirteen-month-old, but it also produces a wet floor, a wet child, and a mess for Mom to clean up. The power of attraction of the toddler phase is easily averted by substitution. Place a similar bowl of water in a mother friendly location—the patio, laundry room or maybe the garage—and let the child have at it. Do this just before bath time or a diaper change. A little hand splashing and getting wet is the novelty. The location is secondary to the child, but primary for Mom.

And what about the preoccupation with the toilet lid? Get clever. You're not going to purchase a second toilet just to satisfy Junior's curiosity with porcelain and wood. You might find instead a small bucket with a lid that he can play with. Something so simple often does the trick; it's a win-win situation for everyone. The bathroom stays tidy, the child gets to explore, and Mom is relieved that the toilet is not the toy of choice for today.

Keep this truth in practice. During the toddler years, often-repeated joyful sensations become less interesting with the loss of novelty. Novelty is what attracts a toddler. Once satisfied, he moves on to other objects. But while he is at the object, a second powerful force keeps him there—*attention*.

Attention is what holds a child in the moment of exploration, whether it is ten seconds or ten minutes. Attention is the power of attraction. *Attraction* is the result of sensory nerves working in conjunction, holding a child's interest to an object. It could be the color of a magazine, the shiny new pen, the odd-shaped lamp or the musical ring of your cell phone. Color, shine, shape or sound—all are in need of investigation.

Curiosity draws a child to an object, attention holds him to the object, and investigation brings the toddler the excitement of discovery and learning. He picks up the item, manipulates it, bites it, points it, throws it, and taps it. The developing brain is working, processing, reinforcing, and gaining usable sensations. This is all part of a young toddler's discovery process.

Curiosity, Mobility and No Touch Zones

As discussed in later chapters, there will be some "no touch zones" around the house that your toddler's curiosity has no claims to. Do not err in over-restriction any more than under-restriction. Balance, balance, balance, after all is the key. Many new objects of exploration can be investigated while you are in attendance, but they do not all have to be explored today.

"But I don't want to disappoint my child or stifle his exploration" is a common concern echoed by young moms. What every mom needs to understand is that such statements are meaningless clichés. They have no context. You are not going to be able to avoid disappointing your child, nor should you be preoccupied with the notion that you should. Rather, train your child how to handle disappointment. You cannot create a conflict-free environment because the nature of the child, his growth patterns, and parental expectations will create conflict. Learn to deal with it. Between 12 and 24 months, toddler conflict must be managed, not censored. More on this is found in our discipline section in Chapter Six.

Chapter Three

The Mind
of a Toddler

Some junior high students huddled around the inside perimeter of a schoolyard fence. A passing psychologist from the local university subsequently suggested that the fences represented unwelcome limitations, and that children would do better with an unrestricted schoolyard. The fences all came down. The result? The children began to huddle in the middle of the playground, because they did not know where the boundaries were.

Boundaries play a role in a toddler's life as much as in our adult life. The psychologist above assumed that boundaries were bad. Yet in this case, boundaries clearly represented the perimeter of security and outer limits of freedom. When the boundaries came down, the students' freedoms were lost.

Boundaries are important for a toddler's development, and in the period between 14 and 40 months, boundaries take on two forms. Physical boundaries, of course, are obvious necessities. How far can little feet travel, and how much can little hands touch? Physical boundaries play a role in matters of health and safety. What you allow your child to touch, and where you allow him freedoms to play, are often based on safety concerns first, and learning second. But there is a second boundary to consider, the neurologic boundaries associated with learning. That is to say your toddler's developing brain sets its own boundaries and has its own way of organizing. Therefore, how the mind is stimulated and how learning is organized are as important as learning itself.

More Than a Bunch of Neurons

Some parents think they can stuff knowledge into the child's developing brain like a butcher stuffs a bratwurst. They think teaching their 8-month-old child math and Swahili destines the child to become a genius. Not so. As well-intentioned as these parents may be, their emphasis is in the wrong place—on knowledge disbursement, rather than developing a healthy infrastructure for learning. Helping to stimulate an efficient knowledge processing system during the critical 14-to-40-month period is a "must-attain" goal for toddler parenting.

There is no debate among educational clinicians that a child's ability to learn is tied to how the brain organizes information and what stimulates thought, ideas, and answers. This is one reason why a toddler's curiosity should not be hindered but rather directed. Any activity that engages a toddler's interest, attention, or imagination is a type of toddler brain "fertilizer." If it provokes a response or investigation, the brain is actively working, growing, and organizing.

"Actively" is used here in contrast to the less-desirable, passive form of learning, i.e., sitting too long and absorbing too many video or T.V. cartoon messages. These activities do not help with optimal brain organization, because learning is passive and not interactive.

Mothers write and commonly ask us if there really is an advantage to reading stories to toddlers and preschoolers. Our answer is, "Yes, of course!" There are many advantages, but not necessarily the advantages most parents think of. Certainly, reading to your toddler creates a physical environment of touch and closeness. Often the child is in a parent's lap, finding security in his parent's arms. The parent is also teaching self-control, encouraging focusing and attention skills, and reinforcing the very productive skill and habit of sitting. The child's imagination is also being stimulated, and new interests are developed as Mom walks him through story-land. Often children's stories possess a moral component, allowing you to teach toddler-age virtues. These are some of the wonderful corollary effects of reading to your toddler.

However, holding a book in your lap and reading, "See the bunny!" cannot be compared with a trip to the pet store or zoo where Mom also says, "See the bunny!" In the world of your toddler's developing brain, the real thing is better than a thousand pictures when it comes to organization. The bunny moves, sniffs with little bobbing whiskers, chews a little green leaf, and hops around his cage. The child's brain is interacting far more with the real thing than with a picture story. It is not simply that there is more brain stimulation, but that the type of stimulation facilitates better organization. More senses are stimulated, including sight, sound, smell, touch, as well as a warm, loving feeling associated with the bunny's furry cuteness.

What are the major differences above? The walking, talking, touching toddler connects better than the sitting, immobile toddler. Common observation confirms that a mobile, exploring toddler learns faster and more efficiently than the child whose feet never leave the couch and whose eyes never leave the T.V. screen. The networking of brain activity connecting mobility and discovery is indeed greater than the type of passive learning where there is only input data but no output of energy or stimulation of all the senses.

What does this mean for *Sesame Street*? This popular children's program debuted in 1968. The Ezzo's children were part of the early social experiment of educational television. *Sesame Street* was entertaining and had some educational benefits, i.e., repetition in counting, reciting the alphabet, and, of course, teaching cooperation. And many children spent many, many hours watching the "Big Bird" with yellow feathers. It may have served three generations as a great program and entertaining babysitter, but it came with a developmental price-tag.

What public education via the PBS network could not do, and will never be able to achieve, is to have a two-way conversation with its viewers. A toddler's language formation, for example, does not develop solely by listening, but with the necessary interaction back and forth between people. Your toddler must have opportunities to talk, interact, and respond.

When a child sits and learns passively from television programming, or the best of "Veggie Tales", he is missing half of the equation. The more hours of passive learning and the less opportunity he has to compensate for this type of linear input, the more disorganized the brain becomes, because the responsive side of the brain is increasingly left unattended.

Please take heart. We are not asking you to throw out your television or burn your children's DVD collection or buy a pet store. But we are encouraging you to carefully monitor the amount of single-direction programming that influences your toddler through the medium of television. Passive learning is not a sufficient stimulus.

Finding the Neurological Balance

We see two dangers involving the wrong measure of stimulation. Too much stimulation used to enhance a child's intelligence pushes the child too fast and does not allow sufficient integration time. Knowledge is piling up because it has nowhere to go.

Child-led random stimulation is a second concern. It is not helpful to allow your toddler unlimited freedom of exploration. While his developing brain may receive plenty of sensory input, the overload short-changes the process of association, assimilation, and organization. Learning deprivation occurs when parents consider a child's impetuous and momentary desires to be the primary method of input. Some child-rearing authors suggest that the best way to teach children is to allow them to explore at will through trial-and-error in an unstructured environment. This theory supposes that parents should only act as facilitators of learning rather than directors and teachers of knowledge. That is not a good idea.

Facilitating a child's learning, and teaching a child are two distinctly different approaches. Trial-and-error self-exploration is inferior to structure, guidance, and proactive teaching. Using trial-and-error learning as the principle source of education, even for a toddler, is time consuming and often produces results that are less than satisfactory. Trial-and-error parenting often creates learning environments that are greater than the intellectual capacities of the child. This only produces frustration and confusion. Furthermore, the inconsistency of trial-and-error learning weakens the child's ability to assimilate new information with old. As a result, the infrastructure that will aid future learning fails the child.

Trial-and-error stimulation and discovery violates the fundamental premise of learning. The home is the child's first learning environment and sets the pattern for attitudes toward people, activities and life in general. Therefore, parents must produce, encourage, and manage a healthy learning environment that provides their children wholesome stimuli, while avoiding overwhelming their senses or allowing any portion of their growing minds to be underdeveloped. Thus, a fitting question to ask is, "What does every child need from his parents?" We believe first and foremost that a child needs an environment suitable for learning and parents who proactively direct their child's education opportunities.

The Learning Process

The cognitive ability of toddlers is amazing. They learn by interacting with their developing world, as long as their developing world does not expand too rapidly. They interpret new experiences in relationship to knowledge formerly acquired, and they do so quickly. That means learning is progressive. Your little person gains understanding faster when new information has meaning in relationship to previous experiences, and when all senses are activated, not just a few.

Routine and orderly transition at each stage of a toddler's development aid the marriage between new information and a toddler's understanding. It is a self-evident truth that learning is greatly and positively impacted by order and routine, and it is negatively impacted by chaos. Orderly assimilation of many perceptions gives rise to the formation of ideas much more readily than unstructured environments. Routine works because it allows a child to revisit an experience over and over again. Observe how often your toddler returns to the same toy.

The child who can associate correct meanings with new experiences is far more advanced in his or her understanding than the child who must associate a new meaning with an old situation that is in need of correction. The latter is a common legacy of *laissez-faire* parenting. Since learning comes in progressive stages, training should take place in the same way. For this reason, parents need to provide their child with a learning environment that matches information with understanding.

The best way to describe this is to return to our *Babywise II* funnel analogy. (While we will reintroduce the funnel concept in this chapter, the practical application is more fully developed in our next chapter, "Structuring Your Toddler's Day.") Please take note of the funnel analogy below.

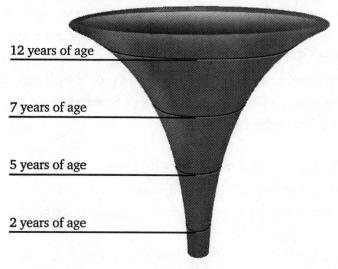

12 years of age

7 years of age

5 years of age

2 years of age

The long stem of the funnel represents the early stages of parenting, while the wider portion represents a child's growth, maturing process, and gradual attainment of freedoms. As the child grows up through the "stem" of the funnel, freedoms are earned to the extent that the child demonstrates responsible behavior.

The most common mistake parents make is to parent "outside the funnel" in the toddler months. By "outside the funnel" we are referring to those times when parents allow behaviors that are neither age-appropriate nor in harmony with a child's moral and intellectual capabilities. To allow a 15-month-old child freedoms appropriate for a 2-year-old child, or a 2-year-old child freedoms suitable for his 5-year-old sister, is to parent outside the funnel. Such freedoms do not facilitate healthy learning patterns—they only contribute to confusion.

Here is the heart of this matter: your desire for the developmental harmony of your child makes it necessary that you grant freedoms to the child only after he or she attains the age-appropriate level of understanding and self-control. A freedom granted a child who is not guided by the amount of self-control necessary to handle that freedom ultimately leads the child to enslavement of his passions. When freedoms granted are greater or less than the child's self-control capacities, a state of developmental imbalance is created. Please consider the following basic equations:

1. Freedoms greater than self-control = developmental confusion
2. Freedoms less than self-control = developmental frustration
3. Freedoms equal to self-control = developmental harmony

The first statement explains that freedoms granted to a child that are greater than the child's ability to assimilate new experiences produces developmental confusion.

The second statement refers to the fact that withholding freedoms from a child who possesses age-appropriate abilities will eventually foster developmental frustration. This usually does not occur during the toddler phase of development but typically shows up in a child of between 5 and 8 years of age. This period is when children begin measuring the legitimacy of their parent-granted freedoms and restrictions against what other children are allowed to do.

In the third equation, we see that developmental harmony is achieved when freedoms awarded a child are appropriate for his or her level of understanding and self-control. When things seem to be getting out of hand, when naughtiness abounds more than self-control, and when defiance overpowers compliance, you might just want to consider the funnel factor. Have you given your toddler too many freedoms too early?

The Toddler Who Had Too Much

Will and Tashia were pleased with the abundance of curiosity contained in their 24-pound, 18-month-old daughter Julia. They figured if a little freedom was good for a developing curious mind, certainly offering her unlimited freedom would be even better. As a result, sweet little Julia had the freedom to come and go without guidance, explore without limits, and touch all without restraint.

When she wandered over to their neighbor's driveway and picked up a discarded cigarette butt, she was very reluctant to give up her new treasure. When her mom tried to pull it out of Julia's fingers, a temper tantrum followed. And what about the episode earlier in the day, when Julia crawled behind the bushes in the backyard, where Will had days earlier sprinkled insect poison? What a scene that was! A curious 2-year-old girl squared off with the health and safety concerns of Mom and Dad in a contest to see whose will would prevail.

And last night at the church picnic, Julia made a delightful discovery of plates of discarded cake in the trash, sitting within easy reach. Nevermind the flies circling the frosting. Fortunately, her adventure was short-lived, but the price of separation was fought valiantly with loud screams, kicking little legs, and plenty of tears.

At some point even little Julia needs boundaries. It is a shame she must go through so much trauma because restraints in her developing world are unpredictable and always "suddenly" imposed. Did we mention the episodes of running in the street, poking the dog with the butter knife, playing in the toilet, ripping pages out of the family photo album, running off with Uncle Jim's cell phone, sticking her Duplo's in the VCR, and turning on the fireplace gas burner?

How does Julia perceive restraints when she has been given all the freedom in the world? All of a sudden, limitations are placed on broad-based freedoms. That equals developmental confusion and creates an unnecessary adversarial conflict between parent and child. No child wants to give up territory once it has been gained.

The problem began when Julia's parents failed to set age-appropriate boundaries during the early days of her mobility. Because of this lack of restraint, Julia's mobility put her in an environment larger than she could manage. The excess freedom created too many new variables that she was not ready to handle. Will and Tashia were parenting outside the funnel. They should have limited Julia's field of exploration by setting age-appropriate boundaries, training her to respect those boundaries, and then allowing restraint to give way to freedom.

Instead, they reversed the process, forcing freedom to give way to restraint. Rather than move her gradually forward toward increased freedoms, her parents kept bumping her backwards with unpredictable restraint. That is not a smart or productive way to parent.

Certainly there will be times when you will recall a prematurely granted freedom because the child is not ready to handle the associated responsibilities. Recalling privileges should not be the norm in your parenting but the exception. You can help yourself avoid this situation by evaluating what you allow your child to play with or do.

Why add a variable to your toddler's life that will only need correction later? Allowing a child unlimited freedom of exploration is developmentally unwise and unhealthy. Freedom is not the problem—the problem is the child's inability to handle the power of freedom. Ask yourself, "Where is my child in the funnel? Where should he be?"

Are you giving your child inappropriate freedoms? If so, parent the constant factors and control the variables until your child has the intellectual and moral capacity to handle the freedoms those variables bring.

Self-legislative freedoms come gradually. In an appropriate amount of time, your child will be allowed to advance from the playpen to the backyard, and then to the neighborhood. As your child demonstrates age-responsible behavior and sound judgment, he will earn another level of freedom. This type of training results in a developmentally healthy child who is a joy to everyone.

Chapter Four

Structuring Your Child's Day

By Carla Link, Contributor

Sondra let out a deep sigh as she watched two-year-old Katie and four-year-old Ben quarrel over a video. She had run errands earlier with the children, stopped to pick up a quick bite of lunch, battled over naps, and now this. Rod would be coming home to a messy house, cranky children, an exhausted wife, and left-over burritos. Sondra bent over as she felt her baby Gregory, growing inside, give her a sharp kick. She wondered in desperation how she was going to handle another baby so soon. As she began to weep in despair she also wondered if all mothers felt this way.

Do you know this mom? Parenting toddlers and preschoolers is exhausting. You might think you need a spare IV bottle next to your bed. Sometimes the fatiguing season of training toddlers and preschoolers might seem to last forever. Let me encourage you. There is something you can do to bring order to your life and sanity back to your parenting, and to help get you get through these wonderfully challenging months.

Mr. Ezzo and Dr. Bucknam introduced the "funnel" analogy in Chapter Three. Their basic premise is born out of a self-evident truth. Most behaviors during the toddler years need to be surrounded, guided, protected, and supervised by the hands of Mom and Dad. A child certainly desires to be autonomous, but is not capable of self-rule at these tender ages.

I had a part-time job while attending college. Each afternoon I went to an elementary school and served as a hall monitor. My job was to ensure all children obeyed the school rules coming and going to and from lunch. The school officials understood that without someone in authority standing there watching, little steps of disobedience could easily turn into giant steps of trouble.

Without supervision, young children tend to choose how they will act based on what they want to do, and not necessarily what they ought to do. Toddlers can no more govern themselves in moments of calm than they can in moments of conflict. This is why parents must monitor their children's activities at home. But what does that look like? You're not going to be a full-time hall monitor for the next twenty-four months. The normal, everyday demands on your time as a mother, wife, daughter, neighbor, and friend will not permit that. There is a way to bring your child's day under your supervision without you lording over the child's every activity. Structure your child's day. Toddlers thrive on routine, just like your baby did.

Structuring Your Child's Day

Elaine St. James, in her book, *Simplify Your Life With Kids*, suggests, "Kids who live without structure can develop behavior problems. Frequent tantrums, whining, a disregard for rules, inappropriate or aggressive behavior, constant demands, and an inability to share are some of the signs that your child needs more structure."[1] We certainly concur with that assessment. The most effective way to provide continual supervision for a toddler and yet provide many opportunities for learning is by structuring your child's day.

To have some routine, order, and structure is to think ahead and plan. Structuring your child's day will eliminate a big chunk of stress on a mother. I often find myself counseling young mothers. I do not regard myself as being old (age of course is relevant to ones view of youthfulness), but I do find myself fatigued after listening to some of the young mothers tell me of their daily plights. I can best describe their day in two words: *random chaos*. Nothing is predictable; nothing can be counted on. Every day is disorganized, hectic, fatiguing, and unfulfilling. There is no sense of accomplishment, except that Mom made it to bedtime and everyone in the house is still alive.

You can easily eliminate much of this confusion, stress, and fatigue by adding some structure and routine to your child's day. Both mom and child will thrive on it. A little planning allows Mom the opportunity to be proactive instead of reactive in her parenting—meaning that she can plan the day rather than reacting to each situation as it arises.

A routine enhances good organization, time management, and provides order. It helps you to achieve your personal goals and your child's goals. Another wonderful benefit of planning your child's day is the reduction of corrective discipline needed. Your child is not finding random trouble because his day is not filled with random freedoms.

---

[1]See Elaine St. James, *Simplify Your Life With Kids*, (100 ways to make family life easier & more fun), Pub. Andrews McMeel, page 172.

Figuring It All Out

There are three natural divisions in the day: morning, afternoon, and nighttime. Within each of these divisions are mealtimes and naptimes. Most parents also have weekly routines and even monthly routines, meaning that some days look different than other days. For example, food-shopping days to your local grocery store might fall on Monday afternoons. Your photo-cropping group falls on Thursday mornings. Then there are the once-a-month reading times at the library, outings with your child's playgroup, and "mommy time" at the beauty salon. Deviation in your routine is quite welcome, but don't deviate so much that you lose all the order you worked so hard to set up.

You may be wondering at this point, where do I begin? What might my day look like? The following suggestions will help you get started.

Setting age-appropriate goals

Taking a peek at Chapter 6, Dr. Bucknam and Gary Ezzo write: "parents need to refocus their thinking from *how* to handle a crisis to the heart of the matter—*why* are they handling it?" They explain that the *hows* of parenting will result from the *whys* of parenting. Why we do what we do is the combination of our beliefs and our goals in parenting.

What do you believe about parenting, and what goals are set for your children? If your long-term goal is to raise a morally responsible, and academically assertive child, than you may find it helpful setting monthly or yearly goals in these areas:

- Moral Training. This category requires continuous education. Moral training develops your child's character through self-control, obedience, manners, patience, sitting, focusing, concentration skills, and relationships with peers, siblings, and adults.
- Academic skills. This requires the development of gross and fine motor coordination, ABC's, mathematics, language, reading, and more.
- Spiritual Training. This relates to Scriptural knowledge, memorization, catechism, or knowledge of historical characters of your faith.

Once you have set age-appropriate goals, devise a workable routine and use your child's wake-time structure to help you achieve these goals. For example, if you want to work on self-control (and who doesn't), you should structure time for your child to sit in his highchair and look at books. Start with a few minutes each day and slowly build up to longer periods. If you are working on sitting skills, or what we call parameter skills (the ability to stay put within a boundary), you might use a four-foot square blanket spread out in whatever room you might be working in. This is great for any child between 14 and 18 months. Provide a few toys but instruct your toddler to stay on the blanket and play until Mommy says its time to get off. This can be worked into your daily routine two or three times a week for ten or fifteen minutes at a time.

Writing Out Your Routine

The best place to start is with writing out your routine. You will find one mom's sample schedule at the end of this chapter. Adapt it to your needs or start fresh. When you begin, consider your personal and family activities including laundry, housework, husband/wife date time, work schedule, and preschool activities. Also, go back and read the early portions of Chapter 6 in *On Becoming Babywise*. Do you remember the two couples? The couple who appreciated tight boundaries and structure, and the couple who recognized the need for some order but were far less regimented? Where do you as a couple fall between these two examples? Make sure your daily plan fits you, and not someone else's ideal.

Take a piece of paper and list for each child all the activities of the week, beginning with meals and naptimes. Then you can add the outside activities, roomtime and playtime activities, and table activities, which might include painting, drawing, pasting, coloring, puzzles, blocks, Duplo's and more. There is also sit-alone time, reading time with Mom, and possibly some video time. You must also schedule in shopping time, lunches with Dad, visits to Grandma, and an afternoon play group. Put it all down.

Once you identify your daily and weekly activities, take a second sheet of paper and divide it into half-hour or quarter-hour increments. Start planning each day. Notice how the weekends differ from the weekdays. You can make your schedule as simple or detailed as you wish. Print it out in color or black and white. Frame it, magnetize it, or tape it to the refrigerator. Its purpose is to serve you in whatever form you create. Have fun.

We only sound one warning. Do not become a slave to your daily schedule. As it was in your *Babywise* days, your infant's routine played a guiding role in your baby's day but it was not the rule of life. Your toddler's routine is to serve you and your child, not the reverse.

Once you consider the various aspects and uniqueness of your family, start sketching your plan. Here are some specific ideas and guidelines.

Routine

What can be included in the morning routine for toddlers and early preschool age children? Where do you begin?

- Set a consistent time for your children to start their day. Most parents start around 7:00 a.m. You might start earlier or later, and that is fine. But you must establish a start time.
- The first rule for happy morning wake time starts 10 to 12 hours earlier. Do not let your child set his own bedtime. You're the mommy. You set the appropriate time. Do not keep him up late at night thinking he will sleep longer in the mornings. Rarely does that work out and usually makes for a cranky child and a challenging day.
- You can teach your children to stay in bed until Mommy or Daddy comes to get them. Even after you make the transition from crib to bed, your toddler should not have the freedom to get out without your permission. To help with this you might consider placing some books by his bed, (after he falls asleep) and tell him that when he wakes up in the morning he can quietly look at the books until Mommy or Daddy comes in to get him.
- Assist your children in getting dressed before breakfast.
- Work with them to put their pajamas away and straighten their beds.

- Feed them breakfast.
- After breakfast start their morning routine.

There are many activities that can take place. So when determining how to structure your child's morning, determine what activities fit your plan for the day, such as:

- **Roomtime**—The purpose of roomtime is to teach your child to learn to play quietly by himself for a period of time. This helps him learn to focus and to play independently without having someone or something there to 'entertain' him. For a toddler between 14 and 20 months, consider starting his time on a blanket. (Some toddlers at these ages might still be enjoying their playpen time; you do not have to rush to roomtime.) On the blanket, give him something he likes to do, such as playing with trucks or a toy farm set. Instruct him to stay on the blanket and play with this toy until the timer goes off. Set a portable kitchen timer for five minutes for the first few days. After several days, slowly increase the time by five minutes working blanket time up to thirty minutes or longer. As the time increases your child's self-play adeptness also increases. One last note related to roomtime: make sure you rotate the toys that your toddler plays with. Gary Ezzo and Dr. Bucknam shared about novelty in Chapter 1. When an object loses its sense of novelty the child loses interest. So whatever you place in front of him, make sure it is stimulating and holds his interest. Rotating his toys will help with this. (See Chapter Eight, "Toddler Topic Pool" for additional information on roomtime.)

- **Free Playtime**—This is when your child has the freedom to choose what he wants to play with. It is still supervised because you are carving out the time slot, but it is free time because the child is making the decision according to his interest. What you are not going to do is to allow him to move from toy to toy every five minutes, but instead to learn to sustain his own interest. Keep his activities broad. For example, your two-and-a-half-year-old might desire to play on the back patio, where he has his big wheel, sandbox, slide, and his toy lawn mower. For reasons of caution, please remember toddlers need to be supervised! Free playtime for the child does not mean out of the general sight for Mom.

- **Structured Playtime**—This is a time when Mommy picks the activity. What you are teaching your child is that he doesn't get to always be the one to choose. It is a valuable lesson for a child to learn early on, for as he matures and goes to school, there will be few things in his day he has the freedom to select. Again, start with a timer and use small increments of time. This activity can include playing with puzzles at the kitchen table, coloring, or painting. It is wise to keep scissors away from little toddler hands.

- **Structured Playtime With Siblings**—This activity can overlap with some of the others. For example, two siblings can be coloring at the kitchen table or playing in the back yard together or sharing reading time. There will be many hours shared with a sibling, and that is why we recommend some "alone" time for each child. While siblings tend to entertain each other, each child must also learn the skill of entertaining himself.

- **Playtime With Mommy**—A time should be structured into your daily routine, preferably in the morning, when each child receives individual playtime with Mom. Even if this is only ten, fifteen or twenty minutes a day, it demonstrates to the child that he is special.

- **Playtime With Friends**—There is value in having time allotted during your week for your child to socialize with other children his age. When dealing with the younger toddler, it is best when playtime is structured and supervised. Besides having a friend over, you might consider attending a story hour at the library, or joining a small playgroup.

- **Video-Time**—Instead of falling into the habit of putting on a video when the children are becoming restless and whiny, learn to structure a video time when it works best for you. Look for a time of day that is most stressful for you, possibly around mealtime or tidy-up time. The videos used during the morning routine for toddlers, we believe, should be limited to a half-hour.

Afternoon Routine

The following are examples of what might be included in your afternoon routine:

- Lunch
- Naptime
- Roomtime
- Structured Playtime with Siblings
- Video-Time

All toddlers and early preschool age children need an afternoon nap. Some younger than 16 months old might need a short morning nap but for the most part your toddler is down to one nap a day. Of course the need for a nap does not always mean a child will want to take a nap. As Gary Ezzo and Dr. Bucknam have already stressed, what a child may want is not always what a child may need. The first sign of crankiness after lunch is an early indicator that a nap is needed.

Most moms schedule naptime right after lunch and plan on a good two-hour sleep. So between lunch, cleaning up and naptime, nearly three hours of your afternoon routine is already planned. Some toddlers need some additional time to fully wake up, so for them plan a quiet activity to transition them back into their routine. This might be a good time for a small juice snack and a short "Winnie the Pooh" video. Other toddlers wake up full of energy; for this little person a trip with Mom to the swing-set in the back yard might be in order. For both types of wake-up moods, after naptime is a great time to run errands, go shopping or visit a friend. Well-rested children do much better in stores than cranky, tired ones.

If there are any school-age children in the house, your toddlers will be excited to see them. Provide some sibling playtime or snack time together. Older children learn that once they have given their younger siblings undivided attention, that sibling is less likely to demand it from them (in a manner that will cause conflict) at a later time.

Evening Routine

The evening routine usually involves another adult on the scene—that being Dad. Every couple sets their own parameters when it comes to Dad and how immediately involved he becomes with the family after work. The one nonnegotiable would be couch-time (discussed below). In counseling young moms who find their day consumed with discipline and correction, I find a relationship exists between the absence of couch-time and the increase in defiant behavior. Couch-time provides a soothing accent to family life in general. After couch-time it might be kid's time or dinnertime, but for sure it should be some form of family time.

What can be included in the evening routine?

- **Dinner**—Mom can plan quiet playtime for the children as she is preparing the evening meal. If Dad is delayed or working longer than normal hours, it is usually wise for Mom to feed the children rather than wait for Dad. The longer young children have to wait for their evening meal the more cranky they will get, and the more difficult mealtime will be. Mom can eat with Dad when he gets home, and if the time is right, the whole family can have dessert together. Remember, evening activities should work towards quieting your children down and preparing them for bedtime.

- **Family Time**—This can include an activity that the entire family can participate in. Dad may read a book to the children, or play puzzles or age-appropriate games. Again, save dessert time for family time.

- **Dad's Time with Children**—Children need undivided attention from their father, even if it is only a few minutes each day. Dad can spend time with one child while Mom is bathing the other children. This may be a short walk around the yard or through the neighborhood, or just going to visit your next-door neighbor.

- **Couch-Time**—It is important that children see their parents getting along. They also need to understand that their parents have a relationship outside of their parenting. We have found that when the husband and wife sit on the couch for ten to fifteen minutes and talk with each other, it teaches the children that Mom and Dad are special to each other. This breeds security in children. Again using a kitchen timer, start with five minutes and build up to fifteen minutes over a period of a couple of weeks. If Mom feeds the children before Dad gets home, then when Mom and Dad sit down to eat can count as couch-time.

- **Bath Time**—Usually bath time for a toddler is a fun time. Have a few toys handy, and of course, never leave a child in the bathtub unsupervised. While bath time is often playtime, there must be some limits. Your child does not need his entire playroom in the tub with him. Little buckets are fun, but the water needs to stay in the tub. Also, limit the amount of splashing or kicking. This is the bath, not the beach or his plastic pool in the back yard.

Bedtime

When we start to think in terms of adding structure into the day, the first place to start is with the children's bedtimes. If I were to ask a mom such as Sondra (above) what time her children go to bed, she would probably without hesitation tell me what time she thinks they go to bed. It has been our experience, however, that what time we think our children go to bed and what time they actually get into bed can be two very different things. I encourage moms to write down for one week the time their children are actually settled into bed for the night. It is surprising to moms when they see that it is a rare week that their children get to bed at the same time, three nights during the week.

Toddlers need 10-12 hours of sleep each night. Therefore, if his day starts at 7:00 a.m., then he needs to be in bed by 7:30-8:00 p.m. each night. It is not uncommon for moms of toddlers and preschoolers to think that when their children are getting to bed at 9:00-9:30 p.m. that this is "early." I often grocery shop late at night and I am always surprised at the number of parents out with very young children. Typically, they are whiny and demanding and the parents are usually threatening and repeating in return. It is unfair to expect overtired children to behave like well-rested ones.

When young children are not getting enough sleep they are irritable, hard to manage, and have little or no self-control. Don't start your day that way. Getting your toddler to bed at least by 7:30-8:00 p.m. each night will lessen the need for discipline and correction. Well-rested children behave better.

If your child's bedtime is currently at 9:00 p.m. or later, begin to work toward your desired goal in 15-minute increments over the next week or two. When we say that a child should be going to bed at 8:00 p.m., we don't mean that you start to put your child to bed at 8:00 p.m. Back up the bedtime routine to 7:30 or 7:45 p.m. Include all the hugs and kisses, story time and prayers. Your goal is to settle him in bed before 8:00 p.m.

Helps for establishing a bedtime routine

- Set a consistent bedtime.
- Avoid TV, roughhousing, and wrestling on the floor with Dad; it will take too much time for your children to wind down.
- Avoid conflict prior to bedtime. This is not the time to get into power struggles. Be directive in your instruction—instead of asking your child if he wants to get ready for bed, tell him that it is time to get ready for bed and go with him to the bedroom to get into his pajamas.
- Whenever possible, hire babysitters when you have to be out at night so your children's bedtime can be as consistent as possible.
- Avoid offering a young child who is being potty-trained unlimited liquids after dinner.
- Consider doing your storytime out on the couch or in your favorite easy chair and not in bed. This is a great time for Dad to be with the child. When storytime is over, off to bed your

toddler goes. Once your child is settled in it should only be prayer time and sleep. If you keep storytime in the bedroom, you never finish because the child has no place else to go; "off to bed" helps cure the habit of "read me another story."

- Experts on sleep disorders agree that it is best for young children to learn to fall asleep on their own. Give him his stuffed animal or blanket, kiss him goodnight and quietly leave the room.

- For your older toddler, have a rule that he may not get out of bed unless it is an emergency. Make sure he understands what an emergency is and is not.

- If your nighttime routine has been rushed or your child gets to bed late because of your schedule, consider playing soft music in his room to help him settle down.

A final word about bedtime—when starting to think in terms of adding routine to your day, start with the bedtime first, then mealtimes. You might be surprised at the difference in your children's behavior when they are well-rested and are eating nutritious meals on a regular basis. Once you have made progress in these areas, you can look to add routine in the rest of your day.

Mealtime

America is raising too many obese children. They load up every day on sugar, fat, salt, and caffeine. Please do not be misled. What your children eat will effect how they behave. If your children are chronically irritable, cranky, whiny, and unmanageable, the solution could be in their diet. To get your child's diet under control, feed him at home.

We encourage you to have regular mealtimes and healthy snacks. Maintain a healthy diet and avoid fast foods as much as possible. Here are some suggestions that can help make mealtime a happy time.

Mealtime Guidelines

- Try to stay consistent with your mealtimes.
- Serve your toddler small increments of food.
- Limit his drink while eating. Fill his cup one-half full and give him that first. When he has eaten his food he may have the other half. Otherwise, a child will fill up on drink rather than eat what is on his plate.
- Don't give him additional servings until he has eaten all the food already on his plate.
- One of the reasons young children are willing to make mealtime a battleground is because they are not hungry. If you are fighting with your toddler and early preschool-age child at mealtime, then you may want to consider limiting the snacks and drinks he gets in-between meals.
- If he misbehaves during mealtime—such as throwing food, spitting, screaming, etc.—put him in a chair in another room to sit for a few minutes to see if he can regain self-control. Inform him that he can rejoin the family when he is 'happy.' When he is calm, bring him back to the table and try again. If he misbehaves a second time, repeat what you did before. If he misbehaves a third time, then he is telling you he is not hungry enough to behave while eating, and he should be excused from the meal. Possibly even a nap might follow. However, if you let him up to play, then that is a victory for him, and every time a

young child gets a victory in this manner, he will not hesitate to repeat the behavior. I encourage moms to have their children sit at the table with their hands folded until the rest of the family is done. Then they may then get up and rejoin the family.

• Work on table manners early on; it is always appropriate to teach young children to say "Please" when they want something and "Thank you" when they get it.

A Word to the Weary

We have provided numerous suggestions to help you establish your toddlers routine. However, many reading this chapter may be feeling overwhelmed at this point. My encouragement is to begin slowly. Begin with one thing at a time, like getting your children to bed at least five nights a week at a consistent time. When you see progress here, start on other parts of your day.

Some people chafe against structure. I was like that. I liked to "go with the flow," wherever the flow was going. But what that earned me was children who were argumentative, whiny, demanding, and not very well behaved. I didn't care for the looks and whispers my children's public behavior brought. I was missing something and desperately needed help. When I was first introduced to the benefits of structuring my child's day, I found it hard to do. It meant I had to gain some self-control in some areas of my life that I didn't want to admit I needed help in.

But today, writing from the perspective of a mother with two teenage daughters and one son in his third year of college, I can speak of the wonderful benefits that came with structuring my day and that of my children. Structure and routine gave me the freedom to do many more activities with my children than I could when I had no routine. It will be the same for you.

It will not always be easy because as moms we naturally wonder if our child is missing out on something. So we begin to add an activity here and another there. Before we know it, busyness controls our schedule. What I learned from my own experience is that toddlers do not need to experience everything over this 36-month phase. You do not need to sign them up for every music lesson, ballet classes, pee-wee soccer, or kinder-gym. They're all wonderful activities, but your child does not need to experience them all. Too many away-from-home activities wear out child and mom.

If you ask parents of college students if they believe the activities they had their children involved in when they were toddlers and young preschoolers advanced them in any way, you will likely hear that they can't even remember them. Having your children in too many activities too early will burn them out emotionally and possibly neurologically. Pick one or two activities for your child to enjoy and let the rest go. (The playgroup and story time at the library are two of my favorites.) Simplify your life.

Whatever Happened to Sondra?

Sondra let out a deep sigh of satisfaction. Her husband would be home soon, and dinner was almost ready. Katie was sitting quietly on a blanket in the family room playing with her dollhouse. Ben was in his bedroom playing with his Legos. The house was picked up. Sondra felt a sense of calm and orderliness.

It had taken several weeks to get here. Sliding the children's bedtime back to 7:30 p.m. hadn't been as hard as she had anticipated, and they were better behaved with the additional sleep. Ben only napped three times a week, yet he was willing to stay on his bed and look at books for rest-time the other days. Both kids dropped the morning playgroup down to once a week, and the only other outside-the-home activity was Ben's junior gymnastics once a week. The children did not complain about missing the other activities. They didn't care. The siblings were getting along better and even looked forward to the times during the day that Sondra had scheduled a joint playtime. It had taken time, planning, and perseverance, but in the end it was all worth it.

Sondra and Rod can spend the rest of the evening as they choose! If Sondra wants to do errands, she has the freedom to do them. She now has the freedom to be a mom, wife, daughter and friend.

Sondra's schedule, next page, looks like this. Take whatever you can use and make up your own schedule from it. Be flexible and remember the first rule of routine—your schedule is to serve you and your child, you do not serve the schedule.

Summary

Years ago, Anne Marie Ezzo did a study on the word "amusement." "Muse," according to Webster, means to become absorbed in thought. The prefix "a" on the other hand, means "not" or "without". It negates an action. Amuse means to avert attention. Mothers too often spend their time simply amusing their children during the many hours of the week rather than proactively ministering to the child's heart and intellect. Parenting takes us down a one-way street

—our children are growing and developing at tremendous rates. There is no rewind button. The goal of parenting is to raise thinking, responsible, autonomous children that who are a delight to you and the community. Such results are not achieved by chance or luck, but

Sondra' Schedule
Illustration 5.1

7:00 – 8:00 a.m. Get children up & dressed; pajamas put away, beds made; enjoy breakfast

8:00 – 8:30 a.m. Free Play Time (Ben, Katie)

8:30 – 9:00 a.m. Structured Play Time (Ben), Free Play Time (Katie)

9:30 – 10:00 a.m. Video Time (Ben), Structured Play Time (Katie)

10:00 – 10:30 a.m. Room Time (Ben), Blanket Time (Katie)

10:30 – 11:00 a.m. Structured Time with Mom (Ben and Katie)

11:30 a.m. – 12:00 p.m. Structured Time Together (Ben and Katie)

12:00 – 1:00 p.m. Lunch, clean up, read books until time for rest/nap

1:00 – 3:00 p.m. Nap (Katie)

1:00 – 2:00 p.m. Rest Time (Ben)

2:00 – 2:30 p.m. Free Play Time (Ben)

2:30 – 3:00 p.m. Structured Play Time (Ben)

3:00 – 4:00 p.m. Gym Class (Ben and Katie)

4:00 – 4:30 p.m. Structured Play Time Together (Ben, Katie)

4:30 – 5:00 p.m. Room Time (Ben), Blanket Time (Katie)

5:00 – 5:30 p.m. Video Time

5:30 – 6:30 p.m. Dinner, clean up, etc. (Mom and Dad have couch time)

6:30 – 7:00 p.m. Family Time with Dad and Mom

7:00 – 7:30 p.m. Time with Dad (Ben), Mom gets Katie ready for bed*

7:30 p.m. Katie in bed

7:30 – 8:00 p.m. Ben gets ready for bed

8:00 p.m. Ben in bed

*On alternate nights, Dad bathes Katie while Ben has Quiet Time

by planning. Structuring your child's day can help you achieve these attainable goals. Take some time and write down a list of possible activities that make up your toddler's week. Design a daily and weekly plan around your activities and enjoy the peace that comes with structure and routine.

Chapter Five

The Land of Good Reason

O pinions on how to raise a toddler are easy to come by. Just type "toddler" into your Internet search engine, and you will find more than 900,000 options. Twenty top listings are highlighted for greater speed! This is great news if you are in a hurry, but which one do you read first? Whose advice will you believe? What options fit your family's identity? By the time you sort it all out, your toddler will be 22-years-old and pouting over a down payment on a house.

The ease with which parents can find a ready-made solution might be part of a bigger problem within our society. Whenever there is a surplus of easily accessible knowledge, there is a corresponding downside—the reduction of critical thinking skills, leading to atrophy of thought. The less skillfully you think, the more others will think for you. From the viewpoints of an educator and a medical practitioner, this chapter might well be the most important for many of our readers. It's not one *filled with* answers to your toddler questions, but it shows you how to *find* your answers. It's not a *"how-to"* chapter but a *"how-to-think"* with good reason chapter.

This chapter is all about problem solving. How do you decide what to do in the moment of toddler conflict or needs? What is the best prescription for your toddler's wandering hands or little feet: encouragement, correction, diversion, or isolation? What play-group should he be in, or what freedoms should he have? How do you know where to draw the line? How do you know you're making the right decision for the long haul? What do you base your decisions on?

This chapter is not about *how* you parent, but *why* you do what you do, and what happens to your thinking when the all important *why* is removed.

Consider these very real toddler scenarios. What if it is your toddler who:

1. Runs toward the street, ignoring your calls to stop.
2. Gets out of bed before you awake in the morning.
3. Pats your newly washed sliding doors with his sticky hands.
4. Cries every time you drop him off at the nursery.
5. Is told to stay out of baby sister's room, but is found climbing the sides of her crib.
6. Is caught taking toys home from the neighbor's yard.
7. Tells you that he does not have to go potty and then messes his pants.

What would you do in each situation, and why would you do it?

The Land of Good Reason

Imagine a faraway land where you face situations with satisfactory solutions, free from self-doubt and second thoughts. This the "Land of Good Reason," where keenly interested parents find rest and encouragement and answers to their toddler questions. In this place where beautiful ideas dangle ripe and the Southern breeze wafts gently, dwell the *Rationals*. These are people who know how to find reasonable solutions to the unreasonable behaviors of the little people living in their homes. The Rationals understand that little people present unreasonable behaviors in need of sensible solutions. This neither alarms them, nor causes distress.

Does the Land of Good Reason seem impossibly unreal to you? It need not be that way. The use of rational deduction to make sound parenting decisions in moments of testing is a tool of reason, and "Good Reason" awaits every parent keenly interested in finding reasonable solutions. As you will read, found within a delightful melody known to all Rationals is the secret of reasoning well.

Over in the Land of Good Reason, the Rational mother tucked in her little wanderer for an afternoon nap. Then she settled back in her sea-green lounger, footrest popped up, to gaze upward and outward through her glass-topped abode. Her windows were open so the breeze drifted through as she hummed a melody she learned as a child.

"Believe in your beliefs," she softly sang. "Trust that your goals are true. Then you'll know why you try what you try. The truth behind effort serves you." Slowly, and rhythmically, the mother, nearly dozing, repeated the sweet refrain. Eventually, and with no particular haste, a most splendid parrot swooped this way and that over the glass-top home, catching the Rational's attention at last. Having alerted her of his presence, the lovely green creature circled down and around to the window ledge next to the lounger.

"Hello, beautiful parrot", she said in greeting.

"Beautiful parrot. Yes, beautiful parrot", he answered on cue.

"Tell me, my parrot, about my beliefs", said the Rational, still dreamy and soft-spoken.

"Beliefs. *Beliefs with goals* equal *why,* add *how* and you come to solve your problems," the parrot rattled.

"Thank-you," said the Rational mother, picturing the formula in her mind.

BELIEFS + goals = WHY + how = Solutions to (toddler) needs.

With this confidence, the Rational laid back and closed her eyes, content with this confirmation of beliefs connected to the problem at hand. "Believe in your beliefs. Trust that your goals are true," hummed the peaceful Rational, enjoying what remained of the day's restful period. "Then you'll know why you try what you try. The truth behind effort serves you."

Not far from the Rationals was the village of the poor *Howtos.* They had their methods, but knew little of *why.* Once, these lovely people shared a common ancestry with the Rationals. But suddenly struck by a devastating storm called *Need,* the Howtos became isolated from the Land of Good Reason. Many of their sages and elders were swept away in a flood of information, leaving the Howtos isolated from the ways of the Rationals.

Lost forever in the storm of Need, the wisdom of old became buried in the sludge of doubt and fear. The storm washed in new seeds of old habits. Soon a forest of habits grew so thick and dense that seldom did the Howtos see the light of day, and seldom did they dare venture beyond their clustered village. No beautiful parrots ventured over to this land, as the canopy of habits was uninviting and the light of day too weak. Instead of thinking for themselves they fell into the habit of letting the council think for them.

One day sitting on her front stoop, a weary Howto mother pondered deeply, "My grandmother used to sing the song of the Rationals. Within the lyrics is the formula that can free me from this forest of Habit. How did that song go?" She mused over the lyrics. "Dream of how to find a solution? Or was it, Believe in your habits? No it was, Dream about your habits. No, no, I must know this song. Ah, tonight I will summon the Council of the Wise."

Impatiently she waited for dusk to settle in over the ridge, and then she took out her wee little fife and beckoned for the council. They swooped in by the hundreds—owls of every size. Some had wide brown eyes encircled with thick white downy feathers. Others were small and brown, plain looking to the natural eye. Some gray ones sat high above the rest, looking down. Eagerly, she asked the multitude of owls to recall for her the parrot's old song. "Please, dear council, might you share with me the parrot's teaching on the little people?" Then respectfully she sat on her doorstep to listen intently, eager to hear the sweet song of old.

"Parrot?! What does she mean, summoning us to discuss some puffed up imitation of guacamole? This woman has nerve," flapped the first gray owl to swoop down before the frightened Howto. "Pipe down, old fool," flared up a larger brown owl, plump and cheerful.

"Don't get those new feathers ruffled. These pitiful creatures count on our, ahem, expertise." Then turning to the Howto woman, he inquired with feigned sympathy, "What is it you want of the parrot's teaching my dear?"

"Well, I..., I..., I just know the sweet peace of the song my grandma would sing as she fiddled with daisies in her garden. I never met the parrot, really, and I don't mean to offend you. I just thought if I could only...," she rambled, her voice weakening and drifting off, lost in the growing grumbles of the council. "Well my dear, if you must know the truth, danger awaits those who think too much. Get everyone thinking, and what do you have? Shambles! That's it. One does this, and another tries that. Before long, they're all reasoning things out on their own. Then, who's listening to the council of experts? Who? Who?"

"Shame on you and your fragile ego," said a distinguished old gray owl. "I know the song of which you speak, my dear. It is the song of the Rationals."

"And how do you know these words?" laughed a smaller brown speckled owl with a trendy tie. "You venture this poor Howto mother to folly. It will do no good. Habits cannot be changed."

The Howto mother glanced up at the thorny trees and sought out the large creature. "Hush, all of you!" he demanded. The gray owl settled in with a bob and a sway, stretched his neck with a twist, and turned and spoke with dignified slowness. "I knew of the ways of the Rationals." He paused. "Their village is close. Before the flood of Need, I lived in their trees."

The forest clamored with hoots. "You have not spoken of this before," piped up a rather dull looking owl with darting green eyes. "And if their village is so close, why have we not seen these creatures?"

"No one asked before," returned the old gray owl. "Their village is just outside the Forest of Habit. No Rational would venture through the foreboding forest, for they know that to do so is to get lost in the way of Habit."

He turned again to the Howto mother. Slowly the song of the Rationals burst forth from the old owl as he swayed on the top branch. Clearly, this was the song of old. "Believe in your beliefs. Trust that your goals are true," he sang to the enraptured Howto. "Then you'll know why you try what you try. The truth behind effort serves you." At this, the forest fairly shook with nervous giggles and grins of fellow owls. Slowly, the Howto mother pondered and then turned, enthralled by her discovery. "The formula!" she called out. "It is there. Beliefs. Goals. *Why*, then *How*. Here in the land of Howto we only know of *how* but not *why*, and *why* comes from the union of our *beliefs* and *goals*."

From one Howto mother to another, the song was repeated again and again, and it caused the old habits to die off. The light of day grew brighter as the canopy of habit pushed back. Soon the beautiful parrots came reciting their wisdom to all who would listen.

"BELIEFS + goals = WHY + how = Solutions to (toddler) needs"

What can we learn from this distant land? While imaginary talking parrots and owls live in the land of enchantment, you and I live in the here and now. But the two villages very much represent parenting styles true to this day. Dwelling among us are the Howto parents, who know much about the way of parenting. They have formed comfortable habits. They have their methods and allow no substitutes. Their mantra is *just show me how*. How do I stop these sticky fingers from touching the clean windows? How do I stop this child from running toward the street? How do I keep this child in his own bed? Once they have the *how*, they never think of the *why*.

The *how/why* Dichotomy

The word *dichotomy* is often used to express a puzzling contradiction. The word actually has a specific technical origin in logic, astronomy, botany, and zoology. It has wrongly been taken over by writers whose only idea of its meaning is tied to fallacies, i.e. *false dichotomy*. The word comes from the Greek *dikhotomia*, a splitting into two, and in English it originally referred to a division into two strongly contrasted parts. This is how we are using it.

We begin with a question. What values or virtues do you deem important? We all work from a hierarchy of assumptions and beliefs. If you were to diagram a personal pyramid of values, what would be at the top of your list? What would be ranked second, third, and so on? What convictions do you hold? What goals do you have for your children, family, marriage, parenting, employment, friends, or matters of spiritual importance? Parenting is made most difficult if the answers to these questions remain nebulous, distant, or unimportant in your thinking.

Once you identify your beliefs and goals, you have the **W** in our equation—the *why* of our behavior. The next symbol of the equation is where the rubber meets the road in parenting. It is taking the *why* behind what we are doing, based on our beliefs and goals and translating it into *how* we accomplish our *why*. In other words, *why* is the value, and *how* represents the many options of application. *How* is what will get you to your goal. Most importantly, *how* has value only to the extent that it can satisfy *why*.

To understand the *how/why* portion of our formula, we introduce a common workplace example.[2] Suppose your supervisor sends you a memo asking for copies of the financial report. He needs the report for the directors, who are meeting right after lunch. You step into action. How will you satisfy the supervisor's request? You probably take the report to the copy machine. Or, if the line is too long, you might take the project to a local copy service downtown. You could even print the reports from your computer. The method used to duplicate the report, the *how*, serves the value of *why*. In this situation, you might ask yourself, "Why am I duplicating this report?" The answer is that there is a board meeting, and you were instructed to provide copies for all the directors.

When *how* Tries to Take Over *why*

One of the most unrecognized causes of frustration in the management of the home or the corporate office appears when *how* takes over *why*. We mistakingly and unintentionally assign value to *how* and then let it supercede the greater value of *why*. How easy is it to let this happen? Let's go back to the copy machine example.

---

[2] This wonderful concept was first shared by Joe Barlow, a friend of the Ezzos. He learned it from his father, Daniel Barlow and his mother Teresa Barlow, who both applied it to the workplace and the successful rearing of their fourteen children.

The supervisor asked you for copies of the financial report. You go over to the photocopier and push *Start*. You process a few pages, and then the red indicator light begins to flash. What will you do? Of course, the first thing we all think of is to fix the copy machine. You open the paper trays, check for jams, remove the jam, and reset the machine. Again you hit *Start*, and again the red light flashes. Frustrated, you open more panels, clear the rollers, check the toner, shake the paper, and start over. Another jam occurs. You call a few friends over to help you. They suggest calling the copy repair service. Now your controlling passion is to fix the copier.

But if we were to stop in that moment and ask, "What was the original *why* that led me to the copy machine?" The answer would be, "To duplicate the report." Is there another way you can duplicate the report? Yes, you can go next door and use the neighbor's copy machine, or as suggested above, go to a copy center, or try printing the copies of the report from your computer.

Here is the point. Sometimes the *hows* of life stop us cold. Out of frustration we begin to examine why our method (*how*) does not work, and we miss moving forward in life because we are stuck on a broken *how*. The secondary *how* then begins to dominate our thinking and consumes our time and our emotional energy. We end up worried and more focused on fixing the *how* than returning to the original *why* to consider other means to satisfy it. In fact, we often become spellbound by fear that if our *how* does not get fixed, our goals will never be achieved.

What does *why* do for us? It keeps us focused on the hierarchy of our values. In our scenario, the greatest value now is not fixing the copy machine but getting the report duplicated and to the directors' meeting on time. The *how* is secondary and only serves the primary *why*.

In parenting the greatest values are not on *how* you accomplish your goals, but the *whys* that govern your goals. *Do not lose sight of the why of your parenting.*

At the risk of repetition, but in hopes of making this point very clear, consider this second personal illustration. Recently Anne Marie and Gary met with their neighbors and friends, Harold and his wife Nancy, at the boat launch on the river. They pulled the boat out of the water and securely cinched the bow to the trailer. The wives moved into the truck to find relief from the swarms of mosquitoes while Harold and Gary went to the back of the trailer to harness the stern. (Tying down the stern is done as an added measure of security when towing the boat.) With mosquitoes attacking their unprotected legs, arms, and heads, Harold, an old-time South Carolina gentleman, took one side and Gary took the other. In a few moments Harold was done, but Gary could not get his cinch hook to tighten. He took the strap off, he examined it, reversed it, and tried it again, all the while swatting at mosquitoes. He still had no luck. Taking the cinch in his hands, he examined it like a craftsman examines a fine piece of wood, reversed the strap configuration, refastened the trailer hooks, and pulled hard. The straps gave way. Harold just stood there looking at him. Gary gave it another try but to no avail.

Then Harold, in his Southern gentleman's way, asked, "What's the problem?"

"Cinch strap won't grab," Gary responded.

Harold's no-nonsense response rescued Gary from the *how* of his situation and met their need to get away from the festering mosquitoes. "Use the stern rope hanging over the side in front of you," he said to Gary.

The stern rope? Why didn't Gary think about that? It was dangling right in front of his nose. It even got in his way once. His frustration with a broken cinch strap prevented him from seeing the obvious. Gary was so consumed with the broken *how* (the cinch strap that had worked effectively before) that other alternatives to satisfy the original *why* (securing the stern) were not even considered.

How easy it is to get caught up in the *hows* of life and let them replace the more important *whys*. Harold's simple suggestion brought Gary back to the original *why* of his actions: to secure the boat.

This unfortunately is exactly what happens in parenting. We get so caught up with methods of parenting that we forget the *whys* of our parenting. We let the servant *how* become the master over *why*, and that locks us into a process of frustration leading to potential failure. The **H** changes the value of **W**, and we can never come to the best workable solution. Caught up in the forest of habits, we find a solution that might work in the moment, but there is doubt, second-guessing, and the lingering thought, *"did I handle this right?"*

Unfortunately, many a mom and dad stop right there—at "How to," which is primarily made up of *how*. These are the Howto parents. For the Howto mother, learned resolutions are everything. Night and day, day and night, she ponders the overwhelming dilemma, asking, "How? Show me how." Incredibly and most clearly, the Howto mom never stopped to consider *why* she was so bothered by the windows smudged with peanut butter. Was the obstructed view such a huge dilemma, or were there other, deeper issues and behaviors of greater concern?

In a recent conversation, a Howto mother commented to Gary Ezzo that she found herself frustrated when spanking her three-year-old, since it appeared to have no lasting effect on his behavior. She asked Gary what she might be doing wrong. The conversation went like this:

> **Mother:** "Spanking doesn't seem to be working. What am I doing wrong?"
>
> **Gary:** "Why are you spanking?"
>
> **Mother:** "Because I want to teach my son a lesson."
>
> **Gary:** "So the why of your spanking is to teach your toddler a lesson?"
>
> **Mother:** "Yes."
>
> **Gary:** "Is there another way that you can teach the same lesson without spanking?"
>
> **Mother:** (Long pause) "I imagine there are many ways. But I never consider other methods because this worked for my other children."

This was not an unloving mom because she spanked, but she was frustrated because she was fixed on this single method and thought it was the only form of discipline available to adjust her child's misbehavior. She placed a greater value on the *how* of resolving the problem at the expense of the truly greater value, *why*. Why do you want to change this behavior? The *why* behind your thinking is what energizes you to do what you do. Thus, when you lose sight of *why*, *how* actually becomes burdensome.

When we do this in parenting and management, we lock out of our thinking many other good options that might, in fact, be better and far more effective solutions than what we are currently using. Like the copy machine example given earlier, fixing the spanking problem became a greater value than her original *why* behind correcting her child—to teach a moral lesson. There are many ways to teach these lessons. She could have tried loss of privileges, isolation, sit time, natural consequences, encouragement, substitution, and many more positive tactics.

The Rationals know that the *how* of a problem is simply the servant of *why*. To get stuck on *how* is to miss the greater value of *why*. Upon examining *why*, this mom would observe at least half a dozen other "how-to" possibilities. A reasonable *how* for resolving these issues becomes clearer in light of this larger view—a view of the forest, not the trees.

Thinking for a Change

There is a simple, workable, and highly effective means by which you as a mom or dad can make decisions that are right for your children of all ages, without the nagging feeling that you are doing something wrong just because you might be doing something different than your neighbor. The Rational mother sang it, the parrot repeated it, the old gray owl knew of it, and the Howto mother learned it. It is expressed in the following formula.

$$B + g = W + H = (S)\text{olutions that satisfy (N)eeds}$$

Does this equation look confusing? Does it remind you of a bad Algebra 1 experience? Take heart. Actually, it is a rather simple equation/formula, in which you will assign certain values to two letters.

The rest of the equation then will become clear and easy to apply. You will assign the value to letters **B** and **g** to produce the meaning of **W**. We can help you with **H**. Put them together, and you will have your solution. Here is the broader meaning of each letter.

B represents your beliefs about the major categories of training. There are seven general categories outlined below that are very much part of your life, and to which only you can assign value. Other areas may be added if you need them.

1. **Morality.** How do I view right and wrong?
2. **Education.** How will I educate my child in useful knowledge?
3. **Faith and Religion.** How strong is my faith, and what do I believe about God?
4. **Family/Parenting.** What is my parenting style? (This could be mother led, father led, a co-regent leadership, or child led.)
5. **Friendships.** What is our family's basis for community and friendships?
6. **Finances.** What are our core values governing earnings, spending and savings?
7. **Children.** What do I believe about the nature of children, their needs, abilities, and capacities?
8. **Other.** Add any other values of your own.

In the preceding equation, **g** represents your goals in parenting. The lower case **g** is not a typographical error. While beliefs may not always translate into goals, goals cannot exist without beliefs. Goals must have a reason to exist. They are predicated on our beliefs. Whether you have one child or a dozen children, formulating and articulating a set of family and parenting goals is essential to knowing where you are going with this child. Where do you want to be next week, next month, next year, or in three years with your toddler?

W is the combination of your personal beliefs (**B**) and goals (**g**). Together they form the reasons you do what you do, the all-important *Why*. *Why* you parent the way you parent is based on the values you believe are important, and what you have determined to be worthy and timely goals for your children. *Why* represents the constant beliefs in your hierarchy of values.

H represents *how*, and addresses the methods by which issues, needs, or problems may be addressed. *How* looks at the many options available to solve a particular need in your child's life. It could be a physical, educational, emotional, moral, or corrective need. *How* represents the various methods used to solve a problem or meet a need. *How* represents the variables of application.

With our short glossary of terms we can now venture into a deeper probe of this life and parenting formula. We will start with the need or problem and work backward. There is a need (**N**) or a problem calling for a solution (**S**) or a decision.

Without any further explanation we can summarize the purpose of this chapter in a sentence. Take whatever you believe about life and turn these values into goals. Let the goals determine your training priorities, and use methods that facilitate your goals while meeting your child's needs. If this all makes sense, feel free to turn to the next chapter. But if you desire a more detailed explanation of how to make this equation work for you, continue reading.

Starting with a question

What behavior are you trying to fix? What decision must be made on behalf of your child? What need must be satisfied? What problem must be solved? Are you trying to figure out how to best redirect misbehavior, such as preventing peanut-buttery fingers from touching the sliding door, or two siblings quarreling over a toy? Are you contemplating an educational need? Should you put your child in a playgroup? If so, which playgroup will you choose? Should you start preschool, or begin homeschooling? Is it a potty training need? Which method will you use, and when will you start? Whatever question you have, whatever need is present, whatever problem arises, you are obviously looking for a solution (**S**). Where will you find your solution?

Beliefs and goals

In the Land of Good Reason, we meet Rich and Julie, a thirty-something couple with three children under age 6. While Rich counsels other Rationals regarding investments, Julie manages the home-front, bearing constant witness to the family's hierarchy of values. Rich and Julie believe their job includes preparing 3-year-old Caleb for kindergarten.

The goal is noble, shaped by the parameters of the couple's goals and beliefs regarding education. Here is a listing of their parameters. They believe:

1. Education is not all book-learning.
2. Parents must educate a child in life skills, health and safety, and morality.

3. Educating character is as important as educating the mind.
4. Teaching a toddler self-control and how to sit is foundational to a good education.
5. Parents should be more proactive in education, less reactive.
6. Parents are teachers of learning more than facilitators of discovery.
7. Parents are the primary directors of early education.
8. Parents should create structured opportunities to learn.
9. Education for children can be fun, but when it is not, children still must learn.
10. Parents should create an environment that fosters a joy of learning.
11. Children should be educated in useful knowledge.
12. At all costs, learning must be safe and age-appropriate and all goals must be realistic.

Rich and Julie's beliefs (**B**) about education govern their children's educational goals (**g**). What is listed above forms the parameters into which their goals and parenting management will fit. If any belief conflicts with another belief or goal, then confusion, frustration, and disharmony will find a way into their lives.

To follow along with that point, consider this example. If Rich and Julie believe they should create a conflict-free home environment for Caleb, while holding to their educational goals, then they will encounter major confusion. That belief would conflict with the following principles, to name a few:

1. Parents are primary directors of education.
2. Parents should create structured learning opportunities.

3. Educating children can be fun, but even if it is not, children still must learn.

4. Teaching self-control to a toddler is foundational to effective education.

Let's say Julie is directing 3-year-old Caleb to sit with her for a story. Yet Caleb, in that moment, prefers to march to the beat of his own drum, both figuratively and literally. If Julie stays consistent with her educational beliefs, then she will work with Caleb to sit still for a story. If Caleb's happiness reigns supreme in that instant, then Julie's beliefs about education fly the coop.

You cannot hold goals (g) that are antagonistic with your beliefs (B) in your parenting. This is the apex, the pinpoint, the exact origin of where parenting frustration and confusion begins. You are serving two masters that are antagonistic in function; one must go. Change your beliefs or change your goals. Rich and Julie's success is due in part to their consistency in beliefs and goals. As long as they stay in harmony, the *why* of their parenting keeps them on track in all areas of Caleb's little life.

It also reduces a tremendous amount of parent frustration. Rich and Julie have a road map and know where they are going and as a result, they have the freedom on some days to take a shortcut or a more scenic route to their destination. That sense of freedom is what reduces fear, doubt, and confusion in early parenting.

Traffic Lights and Chalk Lines

Values, arranged pyramid-style by importance, form a network of convictions that both motivates and restrains parents. They may be likened to a traffic signal: red, yellow, and green, controlling what we allow ourselves and our children to do or not to do at different times. These signals do not change our goals, but they govern how our goals are met.

Every mom and dad has a piece of chalk, figuratively speaking, that they use to "draw the line." The self-imposed restrictions derived from our hierarchy of values establish personal lines of demarcation. These are the nonnegotiable reference points that our goals must fit inside—the "DO NOT CROSS" lines. The question each family must decide is, "Where do you draw the line?"

As important as personal goals are, they must have some moral boundaries. The goal of a successful student is noble. But will it be okay to cheat on tests to get ahead? Is that acceptable to you? Most parents would of course say "No!" without hesitation. They would do so because the goal of academic excellence cannot be achieved outside the nonnegotiable moral parameters. Why is this the case? Because you know that competence and character go hand in hand. You do not want to raise a smart child who lacks integrity.

So, how far are you willing to go to make your child happy? Is it okay if he pulls a few toys out of the neighbor's yard and keeps them in his playroom? Where do you draw that line? Your 2-year-old child finds joy in throwing pebbles in the air, but can he throw them at the house next door? Your child's actions must be monitored for moral liability.

Your Family is Unique

Finally, please understand that all family beliefs and goals must be considered within the context of their own uniqueness. The uniqueness of your family is what creates the variables in parenting. Does Dad work a swing shift? Does Mom work outside the home? Do you use a nanny or have a live-in mother-in-law? Is Mom on call every third weekend? Does Dad work at home or travel for business? Are you parenting your first toddler or your seventh? How many older siblings are doting over your toddler's cuteness? Is your child in day-care or preschool? Are you parenting without a spouse around?

The point is that all families have a different set of circumstances, continually changing and evolving, that influences the way we parent. Families also have different sets of beliefs. Some families let their children watch anything the T.V. offers, while others do not allow their children to watch television at all. Some parents enjoy Santa Claus in the Christmas scene, and some do not celebrate Christmas. The unique differences do not necessarily mean that some families are wrong.

Therefore, solving parenting issues cannot come out of a canned, one-size-fits-all program. You must forge your own answers for the benefit of your family. Your home is not like your neighbor's home. Your lifestyle is different than your sister's. Your beliefs may be in con-flict with those of your parents. Your standards may be different, either higher or lower than your friends. Every home has a set of variables influencing the way a child is raised, and your family is no different.

Summary

To make confident decisions in parenting you need to know:

1. What are your beliefs about the general categories of parenting?
2. What are your goals for parenting?

3. How will you satisfy the why of your beliefs?

The formula, **B + g = W + H = Solutions**, will guide you to your answers. You will be better equipped to solve toddler moments of crisis when you know what you believe, why you believe it, and how you will execute these values. It will get you to your destination without you second-guessing whether your child was somehow emotionally or intellectually short-changed for life. Applied daily, it will keep you in harmony with your beliefs and free from doubts. Enjoy the gentle breeze, and do not lose sight of the *why* behind the *how*.

Chapter Six

Conflict, Training, and Correction

"C'mon, hon, hand over the clicker."

"How about giving me a turn tonight, dear? Give that ol' finger of yours a rest."

"Thanks for your concern. Now hand it over. You know that clicker is mine."

"No. I think it came with the package. Remember that big date night at the home store, sweetheart?"

And so it goes. In general, conflict between two people begin with differing interests. Two parties cannot agree on a point, but, neither party is willing to surrender ground to the other. For adults, these interests are based on specific issues, driven by higher beliefs and values. Many times, when conflict arises, the values-based principle is defended as dearly, if not more, than the original conflict itself. But not so with children.

Unlike conflict in the adult world, conflict with a toddler is driven by the single impulse *"because I want to."* That is because toddlers are not born with moral, political or social interest. Daily conflicts, for them, are not born out of a clash in ideology or moral idealism. They have no sense of common cause, rich or poor, justice or tyranny, right or wrong. In fact, it is his very lack of interest in all these and more that creates the conflict at the start. He is not old enough, wise enough, nor experienced enough in life to sufficiently govern himself. Thus, his interest will not always be most appropriate, his pursuits will not always be the best for him, and his points of attention will not always be the safest.

There will be conflict with your toddler. But it is not a matter of finding moral equilibrium between two diverse expressed points of view (toddler and parent), but rather training and insisting on a way of life that has meaning to Mom, Dad and the rest of society. Toddler conflicts are moments of opportunity to guide, direct and shape his thinking, and to point him in the direction of responsible living.

Me, Myself, and I

That's how your toddler is wired. That is all he knows and that is where your training must begin. Your toddler will not find your fatigue a matter of interest. Your current cold or flu is not a consideration, and your broken perfect fingernail is merely a passing intrigue. Me, myself, and I are a constant refrain. You must take a child from his native state of me-ism and move him to the social state of we-ism. Conflict plays a shaping role in the process.

Used here, the term *conflict* does not denote bad, wrong, disagreeable or poor performance but rather descriptively denoting new awakening, experiences, and sensations in need of assimilation. There are social and family virtues and values looking for a home in the heart of your child. Conflict between his little world and yours is born out of the numerous social adjustments, limitations, and expectations taking place that often collide as he sheds his old infantile view that it is "all about me." He is now moving into a world that is all about "we."

The *me, myself and I* of infancy is gradually transitioned to a family, community, culture, and world of corporation, fairness, sharing, otherness, and patience. The process goes like this. Between 14 and 40 months, a toddler's intellect matures sufficiently to allow meaningful interaction with adults and other children. As that interaction begins, the child starts to process new experiences and sensations that have real meaning to his life. He begins to taste and test new sensations of pleasure, pain, enjoyment, and frustration. He is confronted with gender roles, social norms, family expectations and standards of conduct by big people. A toddler not only begins to perceive how and where he fits into Mom and Dad's world, but also develops a perception of where everyone else in his perceived neighborhood belongs, including brother or sister, grandparents, and the little boy next door.

He is cast into new social settings. He learns not just new rules, but the meaning of rules and observes how other children follow them. He is told to share, talk nice, get in line, stay seated, be good, and be gentle with the cat. There is a heap of learning taking place in a toddler's world because it is not easy for him to figure out what those actions look like in practice. Everything must be experienced firsthand to be understood.

The very nature of toddlerhood mandates that parents place a healthy emphasis on keeping their child on track. Because your toddler has no functioning conscience (meaning he does not possess a working knowledge of right and wrong), you are obligated to make value judgments and moral decisions on behalf of the toddler. This means that external pressure is necessary to bring about acceptable behavior, even though the child has no understanding of the reason for the behavior. The fact that a child has no moral understanding why taking a toy from his sister is wrong, doesn't mean parents should sit back and wait until his moral intellect catches up with moral actions.

The transition between action and understanding is, in part, what makes the toddler years so hectic for young moms. There are numerous antagonistic forces at work. For example, a child needs constant supervision, but also needs the freedom to explore. Likewise, he needs boundaries, yet he needs ample opportunity to let his curiosity take him were it will lead. Equally, he needs to learn when you are ready to teach, but you must be ready to teach when he is ready to learn. We trust, by the end of this book, you will have this figured out.

Where Are You Going?

A woman sipping a can of cola sits by the pool taking deep breaths in between nervous glances around the swimming deck. Every few moments she would grab the can and take a long gulp. Then, like a bull released in a rodeo, she'd charge into action breaking up altercations between her three children. This woman epitomized a frazzled and frustrated existence with no end in sight.

Some parents simply exist. They have no direction, no goals, no plan other than what is pressing in the moment. These are parents mesmerized by the vacuum created by the absence of direction. Not only do they not know where they are going in their parenting, they're usually not aware that they need to be headed someplace. In contrast, *Toddlerwise* parenting is linear in purpose. These parents are going somewhere with their children. They are taking them from point A to B, moving the child from what he is to what he should be with a four-fold goal in mind—to touch the child's moral, emotional, intellectual, and physical capacities in preparation for life.

We do this because children are not endowed at birth with self-control, nor has a toddler lived long enough to know how to make wise decisions. Toddlers need their parent's guidance and self-control. Therefore, parents fulfill the roles of teachers, leaders, and mentors as they guide their children to correct responses and correct thinking. Guidance is most needed in the early phases, when the foundations are being laid in the life of these children. If a child is put on the right track at first and encouraged to remain there until he becomes accustomed to it or learns that it is best, he is less likely to drift to the wrong track later.

Where will you place your emphasis? Think about it for a moment. Where do parents focus most of their training energy? With toddlers it falls into four arenas: health and safety, life skills, moral training, and teaching submission to mom and dad's leadership. The latter is the superintending force that makes the other three manageable.

Parents certainly desire to protect their little ones, so health and safety concerns take up many minutes of the day. There are things we let our children do, places we let them go, and objects we let them use for play. Conversely, there are activities we would never permit them to participate in, places we forbid them to go, and objects that are far, far off-limits. Why do we place such limitations? Because your child is neither old enough, wise enough or experienced enough in life to manage his own safety. Mom and Dad are the health and safety monitors for their children.

We also spend a considerable amount of time teaching life skills. We teach our toddlers shapes, colors, letters, and how to stack blocks. We play and read to them, facilitate curiosity and stimulate learning. We help them acquire useful knowledge to build their life around. We also spend a number of hours per day in the moral arena teaching children how to get along with others, develop community and social skills, *how* and *why* to make wise moral decisions.

But what about the fourth area? For the mobile toddler up to four years of age, parental leadership must be established and maintained or you jeopardize your influence in the other three areas of development. The child that doesn't listen to Mom inside the house is not going to listen to her screams to stop when running toward the busy street. The child that shows contempt for all parental restraint will not hesitate to put himself in harms way if his impulse carries him there. At some point parents must take that big piece of chalk, draw the line, stand with arms folded and declare with resolve, "You will not go beyond this point!" Where you draw that line is up to you, but here are our thoughts on the subject.

The Role of Mom and Dad

When 20-month-old Kara, disappointed in the snack placed before her, pushed her plate off the table, her mom and dad knew she had just crossed a huge line. Firm boundaries were sorely lacking.

As your child grows, so also grows his or her need for guidance. Part of your guidance comes by way of encouraging right behaviors and responses and part comes by correcting wrong behaviors and responses.

Just the thought of it can cause anxiety. Correction can be hard for a parent of a young toddler to even think about using at these tender ages. That is because cultural correction is often linked to punishment suggesting that your child has done something terribly wrong. But that is not usually the case and is rarely so during the toddler phase.

Correction simply means to realign or bring back from error. While encouragement keeps a child on track, correction helps to bring him back on track when his little hands or feet wander off to places they should not be. In this chapter we will limit our discussion to corrective strategies for children between twelve to twenty-four months of age.

Since the principle function of child-training is to teach responsible behavior, parents educate by teaching them what is expected of them. We guide our little ones by encouraging right behavior and discouraging wrong behavior. In this way inner growth, self-control, and the habits of the heart are formed.

Unfortunately, many parents consider discipline to be a means of controlling a child's actions at any given moment. It is that, but that is only part of the equation. The primary objective of early discipline is to lay a foundation upon which the next stage of development can be built in three areas of life: 1. skills 2. health and safety, and 3. moral conduct.

Training that Counts

The mother of two young boys, just one year apart in age, purchased identical toys for both kids every Christmas. So greatly did she despise the conflict that personal gifts and variety introduced, that she neglected both her children's individuality and social development. That is frightening.

For some theorists, parenting is a matter of facilitating a child's natural and impulsive way, rather than actively directing the child's ability to make right decisions benefiting others. Reactive in nature, this nondirective approach seeks to manipulate a child's environment in hopes of making parental supervision non-adversarial. Yet, leadership by nature requires that you make decisions based on what is best and right, not what is perceived as most pleasing in the moment. The same holds true in parenting.

As a mom or dad, some of your simple decisions and instructions will be opposed by your child. So, what will you do? Sit back and wait for the child to "outgrow" the behavior, overwhelm the child with your might and will, or train the child in right patterns of conduct and habits of the heart? We trust for your child's sake that it will be the latter.

There will be many times when your developing toddler will reject or strongly oppose your reasonable instructions. Usually, this is because he is not developmentally capable of understanding the reasonableness of your instructions. For example, all of a sudden a new behavior appears. Your fourteen-month-old is starting to stand-up in his highchair. You instruct him to sit down but he ignores your instructions. There are three influences at work here. First, the child's misplaced confidence in his own abilities. Second, his inability to understand you have a vested interest in his safety and third, there are no such *"all of a sudden"* behaviors in toddlerhood.

All of a Sudden

We know from experience that rarely does a problem with young children develop *"all of a sudden"*. *"All of a sudden"* is what trouble and potential danger looks like. What *"all of a sudden"* does is reveal the gaps in our training that are already present. We just don't catch the little things until *"all of a sudden"* becomes a big thing that scares us. In this story, the toddler's decision to ignore Mom's call to "sit down" did not *"all of a sudden"* appear. It's been occurring on many other fronts during the day, in many ways, but none of which scared Mom as did a wobbly toddler in a highchair. The good news is, she now understands that her child's compliance in these early months is necessary as much for health and safety reasons as it is for moral ones.

To help avoid the *"all of a sudden,"* parents need to be anticipatory. To avoid the scary highchair scenario, work on teaching your toddler what obedience looks like. This task is not as difficult as it may appear. True obedience is often more difficult for the parent than for the child. That is because children always respond to parental resolve and expectations, whether they be high or low. By obedience, we don't mean the yielding that results from repeated threats, bribes, or manipulation of a child through the fear of losing parental love.

Worse than these methods is that of adult persuasion. You cannot govern your toddler by a persuasive argument. Your toddler is a toddler, not your moral or intellectual peer. Attempting to reason with an eighteen-month-old is more of a commentary on the parent's IQ than the child's. Such intellectual gymnastics are not commendable. Lead, direct, and guide your toddler in the confidence of your wisdom.

Principles of Instruction

All training begins with parental instruction. When we consider the role of instruction in early parenting, there are a few facts and elementary principles that can serve as a guide to success. Following these basic guidelines can prevent stress and increase voluntary compliance. Failure to embrace them will lead to unwelcomed power struggles and battles of the will.

Principle One: When you speak to your child in a way that requires an answer or an action, you should expect a response. Children will rise to the level of expectation of their parents. Too many parents expect little and receive exactly that. We find consistently that obedience training is far less of an adjustment for children than it is for their parents.

When we talk about obedience with two-year-olds, let us make very clear what we mean. Obedience for this age-group means that a child complies with your instructions at least sixty percent of the time. Do not misunderstand this point, we are not saying sixty percent compliance is acceptable but rather you are working toward total compliance sixty percent of the time. This figure changes as the child grows. By the time he reaches three it should jump to seventy percent. By age five it should be at eighty-five to ninety percent compliance.

Why sixty percent for young toddlers? The walking, talking, and exploring toddler is in process. He cannot give you one hundred percent obedience because he is not capable of doing so. Later in this chapter we will touch on the capacity issues associated with correction and obedience. That section will bring further clarity to our sixty percent recommendation.

For now it is enough to warn you that if the bar is set too high, too early, it will only lead to frustration for you and the child. If there is no bar or it is set so low that it doesn't require anything of the child, such positioning leads to an out-of-control child that lacks the social foundations necessary for healthy, relational transitions during the preschool years. Start with sixty percent obedience and gradually in time, work up from there.

Principle Two: With toddlers, you must give instructions, not suggestions. You do not need your child's permission to be the mother or father. You are the parent. So avoid asking your seventeen-month-old if he would like to go to bed. If it is bedtime, put him to bed with all the kisses, hugs and prayers you want to give. Just know, bedtime is not the child's option. Neither is leaving the playground, coming to the highchair for dinner or wearing shoes in a clover-filled yard. In that case, stepping over the line could bring the wrath of a stinging bee.

Principle Three: Healthy discipline is always consistent. When you draw the line, stay with it. The child brought back on course consistently is far better adjusted than the child whose discipline is inconsistent or incomplete. Consistency provides security and freedom. The child knows what is expected and what is off-limits. In contrast, inconsistency produces insecurity, and because the boundaries are always in question, it stifles a child's learning and his learning potential. Consistent discipline helps the child to learn there is moral orderliness in the world; certain behaviors will always be followed by disappointing consequences or punishment, and other behaviors will be followed by praise and encouragement.

Principle Four: Require eye contact when giving face-to-face instruction. Here is something you can begin between twelve and fourteen months. This will help your child focus on your instructions and help him better process each instruction. Initially it could involve gently taking your child's face in your hand and directing it toward you, accompanied by the statement, "Look at Mommy's face, Katelynn". Do not give your toddler instructions without first getting her attention. The child who is allowed to look around rather than at Mom or Dad as instructions are given often struggles with compliance because her attention is divided.

By sixteen-to-eighteen months of age, start requiring a "Yes, Mommy" after you give instructions. Initially you might just get a head nod, but it is the start of a wonderful habit of the heart. So, when eighteen-month-old Katelynn is trying to unbuckle herself from the highchair, you would say, "No Katelynn, Mommy will unbuckle you. 'Say, Yes Mommy.'"

Of all the practical helps we can offer, this one has undoubtedly the most impact on a child's developing understanding of compliance. This tool in toddler training serves a two-fold purpose. It will help form the habit of the heart in response to your leadership instructions and also create a heightened sensitivity to your leadership role in your toddler's life. Both are going to be needed once the child crosses over to the "negativity phase" period at two years of age.

Directive and Restrictive Instruction

Paralleling a child's increased mobility is their mental aptitude for understanding basic instructions. Not only does the child understand, he is capable of learning how to respond appropriately. Parental instruction is either directive (telling a child what to do) or restrictive (telling a child what not to do). Both types require a response of immediate compliance and are achievable because of the child's ability to understand. Don't underestimate how early that skill is developed.

Directive Instructions

Directive instructions require a response. That response is trainable. Parents can start calling attention to a right response as soon as their baby begins to show signs of mobility. For example, as soon as baby Megan begins to crawl, call her, then walk to her, pick her up, take her where you want her to go, and then verbally encourage her by saying, "Good, Megan. You're learning to obey Mama." This helps your child become accustomed to your command voice and your praise voice that accompanies the right response.

As your child becomes more mobile and you sense they grasp the concept of coming, then require obedience. That will be achieved by the combination of such words of encouragement as these: "Good boy, Ryan. You're obeying Mama." Obedience can also be encouraged by applying one of the four age-appropriate methods of correction found on page 102.

Restrictive Instructions

Your twelve-month-old can understand basic restrictive instructions. Simple commands such as "stop," "no," "do not touch," or "do not move," are usually the first restrictive commands of early parenting. To bring meaning to those words, "stop" must mean stop, "no" must mean no, "do not touch" must mean do not touch, and "do not move" must mean do not move. This also means parental resolve is required.

What Behaviors Need Correction?

We already defined correction. It means to realign or bring back from error. While encouragement keeps a child on track, correction helps bring the child back on track when his little hands or feet wander off to places they shouldn't be. The corrective side of training is guided by certain fixed principles. These are the fundamentals of correction, the filters through which all corrections must pass. First parents must recognize what things should be corrected. Because we all parent the three arenas, *health and safety, life skills*, and *morality*, you will correct in these three realms. The good news is correction in each arena calls for the same techniques.

Before we turn our discussion to discipline methods, we offer a word about your toddler's understanding of right and wrong.

Capacities and Desires

Childhood correction must align itself with age-readiness. For example, at three years of age, a child's higher conscience begins to develop and is ready to receive moral explanations. Because the child is intellectually ready to understand the "otherness" meaning of moral instruction, "do not hit," "do not steal," "do not lie," parents take on a much greater proactive role in virtue training. They begin to add moral explanation to their instruction in the process of building the child's moral warehouse. However, in light of the absence of moral readiness, parents prior to three years of age predominately work on the habits of the heart. That is, they help their children become familiar with right actions even though he is months away from understanding the moral implications of his own behavior.

What are the developmental implications of these factors? It means predominately that a child under two years of age is acting out of his *nature* and not a moral sense of right and wrong. He clearly demonstrates a *capacity* for wrong, but not the *knowledge* of wrong. While taking a toy from another child in the nursery is a "moral violation" and is a "moral action" that must be corrected, it is only a moral crime for the parent and not the child. Parents are morally responsible because the child is not. For the one-year-old plus, it is simply the operation of his nature. He looks, he sees, he wants, he takes. He does not sit back and contemplate the rightness or wrongness of an action because such behavior for a one-year-old is valueless (*me, myself and I* are dominate thoughts), while at three years of age behavior becomes value-driven.

The responsible parent will of course seize the stolen toy and give it back while instructing Tommy, "You do not take Sissy's toy, that is unkind." In this way, parents are establishing the habit of the heart by establishing the moral boundaries of his behavior through restrictions. At three, he will intellectually be ready to understand the moral implications of stealing, but not at eighteen months. As stated, while a child has the *capacity to do wrong*, he does not necessarily have a *desire to do wrong*. A child's desire to do wrong can only exist when there is the *knowledge of wrong*.

Just as a sidebar, this developmental truth is one of the great evidences found in early Christian writings. One of the New Testament writers presents this very point when he said, "I would not have known sin (wrong), except through the law. For I would not have known covetousness unless the law had said, You shall not Covet"[3]. When you filter out the old-style language you come to the modern translation. One does not know wrong until the standard of right and wrong has been brought to bear on the mind, and so it is with our children.

With children, resident knowledge of wrong begins to manifest itself around three years of age during the early formation of the higher conscience. Prior to that developmental milestone, a toddler operates strictly out of capacity, not desire, and toddler correction must reflect this reality. However, while the child may not understand the moral weight of his wrong behavior, parents do and thus are responsible for correction. You are the child's moral sensibility until he gains it for himself.

Correction for your toddler should predominately focus on redirecting and restricting behavior and not on punishment. The sole purpose of punishment is to set a value on the wrongness of behavior and is something that we will take up in *On Becoming Preschool-Wise* for ages *three to four*.

---

[3]See Apostle Paul's comments. Book of Romans Chapter 7: verse 7, New Geneva Study Bible.

Childishness versus Defiance

Here's the good news. Most misbehavior that flows from a mobile toddler between the ages of one and two years is not malicious in nature. The child is not acting out of heart viciousness or corruptible intent. Yes, he wants to rule himself and that alone can put him at odds with Mom and Dad, but his rulership, while self-serving is not moral in nature, it is developmental. Most of what you will be dealing with at these ages is classified as *childishness* and not, as a general rule, open and willful defiance. Willful defiance shows up in full force around two years of age.

The term *childishness* refers to innocent immaturity. This includes the nonmalicious, nonrebellious, accidental mistakes our children make, including spilling their milk, banging the coffee table with the remote control, drawing on the wall, leaving cookie crumbs around the house, stepping in Mrs. Smith's new flower bed, picking flowers from the public park and whatever else your toddler dreams up. Our children also make unwise health and safety decisions. Oh yes, they can quickly put themselves in harm's way. Climbing the wood pile, standing in the highchair, playing with a broken piece of glass, putting nonedible items in their mouth like Uncle Jake's cigarette butt, and playing near the street, all represent health and safety concerns. That is why toddler's need correction, restriction, and redirection, and a willingness to submit to Mom and Dad's leadership.

Methods of Correction

What tools are available to you for toddler correction? Here is a check-list of options.

Redirecting: The idea here is to redirect a child's attention from what he is doing, which might be wrong, dangerous or unwise, to a new activity.

Isolation: This takes the child beyond simple redirection. Children by nature are social. Isolation means temporarily taking away the privilege of social contact. If he is disruptive in his play group, isolate him to another room. If at home, isolate him to his crib, bed or a chair. With screaming fits and temper tantrums we recommend you isolate the child to his crib or bed. 'The child may get out of isolation when he is calm and happy.'

Natural Consequences: A toddler's mischievousness sometimes produces its own form of natural consequences. The child that teases the dog with his ice cream cone will learn a valuable lesson when his double scoop of Chocolate Crunch becomes the doggie's dessert. When Mom gives a stop command, only to observe the eight-month-old continuing on a collision course with the wall, the natural pain of disobedience is your child's tutor in the moment. You will tend to use natural consequences as your child moves closer to two years of age than in the earlier phase.

Loss of Privilege: This is akin to isolation and natural consequences. Here the child loses a right to play with a toy or a friend because of misuse or misbehavior. The privilege must have some meaning in the life of your toddler in order for it to feel like a loss of privilege.

Naptime: This is not a misplaced paragraph but a proactive method of correction. There are some defiant behaviors that are actually only symptoms of other problems. As a result, parents tend to treat the symptoms and not deal with the root cause. They focus on the outward actions rather than the real need. Temper tantrums, for example, are often the result of an over-stimulated child in need of sleep. The action of the tantrum should be considered secondary to the real problem. It is not discipline that the child needs, but rest. Have you ever seen a well-rested child throw a temper tantrum? Think about it, it is very rare. Recheck your daily routine. Is there something going on that is wearing your toddler's batteries down? How much extra activity is going on in his little life outside the home? Is he getting enough sleep?

Other: This category is what works for you. Of course there are other discipline methods used throughout the ages and there may be one or two more that fits into your family's value system. Like all the above, no single method is always right and no single method is always wrong, but each method should be used with an abundance of graciousness and love.

Summary

Keeping that little person on track is the goal of discipline and bringing him back to where he should be is the role of correction. For his protection, welfare, and the welfare of others, parents must be proactive in the directing and redirecting process. It will be a great error to sit back and let your toddler direct his own show. He needs direction, and yes, correction. Both are demonstrations of love.

Chapter Seven

Potty Training Made Easy

"*F*or everything there is a season, a time for every purpose under heaven." (Ecclesiastes 3:1) The year was 1970 when popular folksingers Chad and Jeremy drew upon this ancient Hebrew proverb for one of the biggest folk-hits of the decade. Maybe they knew what we know now. The seasons of a child's life will set the various seasons for our parenting and offer us predictable timetables for training children. Perhaps as Chad sang about time and purpose, his very soul was wrestling with the profound issue before many of you: Is my child ready to use the potty?

Potty training readiness for a child happens sometime between the ages of 18-to-26 months. However, a more important issue of readiness focuses on Mom and Dad. No other issue in early parenting extracts quite the intensity of potty training. Just the casual mention of it evokes haunting memories and emotions similar to going to a dentist who doesn't believe in Novocain. Potty training is one of those tasks that must be achieved, is not always pleasant, and produces a range of emotions from fear, frustration, discouragement, and anxiousness to accomplishment, peace, satisfaction and joy when achieved. While successful potty training itself is not a milestone marker in a child's life, it is an important transition for child and parent.

Consulting the Real Experts

On a computer, do a search using the words "toilet training". You will find at least 20 websites out of 425,000 possibilities on the subject. There is obviously much talk and concern about this subject. Clearly, an assortment of opinions exists. What was once a common transition of childhood, somehow has became the cornerstone of some interesting psychological theories. Sigmund Freud (the Father of Psychoanalysis), postulated that any conflict involving potty training would negatively impact the developing psyche of the child. We're not sure what that would look like in practice since there are very few examples of abnormal bathroom behavior among the world's adult population today.

Other voices piggybacked on Freud's assumptions adding to a growing social paranoia about a process that has in our opinion, more impact on the parent's psyche than the child's. Pediatrician Terry Brazelton (who is accused of having commercial interest for appearing in super-size Pampers ads) encourages a "let them take their time approach", while popular columnist John Rosemond advocates training them by age two.[4]

In the final analysis the views of Dr. Burton L. White take center stage. He writes ". . . Such theoretical analysis (*referring to Freud*) have never been supported by evidence." He goes on to explain that "Given what we know today, no justification exists for elaborate,

---

[4] "Two Experts Do Battle over Potty Training," Erica Goode, *New York Times,* Jan. 12, 1999, p.1.

treaties of dire concern about toilet training. It is simply one of a large number of necessary chores that are required of all parents.[5]" While Dr. White's statements were made eighteen years ago, Dr. Bucknam believes his words reflect the mainstream views of practicing pediatricians today.

The no nonsense fact is that potty training is just one of the many skills a child learns early in life. It is however, different from the developmental stages our children pass through since parents have a much bigger role in potty training than they do in skills such as walking, talking or chewing solid food.

Many different sources, all wonderfully qualified to be experts, shaped the potty training constructs in this chapter. We drew heavily upon moms whose success in this area of training qualifies them to speak on this subject as much as any theorist of the past or present. While they all had a common goal, moving their toddler from diapers to daytime and nighttime dryness, they equally employed a variety of methods, all of which had a single common starting point—*developmental readiness*.

Developmental Readiness

Developmental readiness is nature's objective marker. It's time to begin. As such, it is much more reliable than any human idea. Readiness speaks primarily to the brain and body's ability to perform a function. There must be certain physical attributes available in order for a child to complete the task as well as a volitional readiness. Between 20 and 26 months, the door of opportunity is open to you.

---

[5]Dr. Burton L. White, *The New First Three Years of Life* (NY: Simon and Schuster, 1985) pp. 325-6.

Pushing a child before he is developmentally ready only creates exasperation and confuses the process. Putting training off until the child is three or older might also work against the training process. Waiting too long can potentially create opportunities for unnecessary power struggles. Decide what is best for you and your toddler, but know a window of *optimal* opportunity does exist.

A child's readiness is one thing, but it must be matched by Mom's readiness. It is important that you do first things, first. Before you begin potty training make sure things in your life are in order. Consider your family's routine. Is your day structured? Do you have regular meal and nap times? Taking time to get these things in order before you begin will help you eliminate false starts. Here is a checklist to consider of the five general areas of readiness followed by five specific signs to look for and work towards.

Bladder Readiness

Most toddlers develop the ability to control their bladders consistently, on average between ages 20 and 26 months. Some may achieve readiness sooner, by 18 months and some may not until 30 months or longer. Some signs of bladder readiness include:

1. Your toddler is staying dry for two or more hours at a time.
2. Your toddler is stopping an activity while urinating or having a bowel movement in his diaper.
3. Your toddler desires to imitate parents or siblings using the toilet.

Other readiness cues include the following:

Gender Readiness

We often hear mothers comment that girls were so much easier to train than boys. The fact that girls tend to show signs of readiness sooner might contribute to this conclusion. Girls typically develop bladder readiness between 18 and 26 months of age while boys achieve readiness between 20 and 30 months of age. Finding success in the early training of a daughter does not mean the same success with boys. Boys can train just as fast and in many cases faster than girls, but not necessarily earlier.

Day and Night Readiness

Once readiness is achieved, daytime bladder control becomes a trainable learned skill. Nighttime bladder control however, is largely developmental. There are things we can do to help our child stay dry at night, such as limiting fluid intake after dinner and encouraging him to empty his bladder at bedtime. You also need to wait for a child to develop enough bladder capacity to hold him through the night, and develop the ability to wake when his bladder is full.

Instructional Readiness

Equal in importance to the physical dimension of readiness is the child's understanding of instructions and demonstration of his willingness to comply. A child who refuses to follow instructions for tasks he understands will probably not follow instructions for a task he has never experienced. Evaluate for yourself. How would you rate your twenty-month-old? Is he characterized by submissiveness to your general guidance during the day? Does he eat what you serve him and is mealtime normally a pleasant time? Will he stay put and play on a blanket for fifteen minutes at a time? Have you been working on sitting skills? When you say, "don't touch", does he comply? Does he obey your instructions to come to you when you call his name at least 60 percent of the time?

If you are able to answer "yes" to these questions, potty training will not only be easier but can be accomplished within a day. If "no" was your dominate answer, you can still potty train, but the process will be more difficult and take much longer. This is all based on this simple self-evident truth—if you have to fight just to get your child's attention, and then do further battle to keep him focused on a task, potty training will not be easy because the process requires a measure of success with both skills.

What can help? Review Chapter Five, "Structuring Your Child's Day". Potty training will come easier if his day is manageable and predictable. Potty breaks, a new activity for your toddler will be easily assimilated into his thinking and become a habit if his day has some structure and routine.

Mommy Readiness

Once you have assessed the child's readiness, it is important to access your own. Do you have the resolve to see it through? Avoid false starts! Like so many other challenges in parenting, planning and perseverance aid success. Children pick up cues from their parents and if they sense that you are not committed to this process, they will respond accordingly. While there may be unique and unplanned circumstances that put a temporary halt on your potty training, such interruptions should be the rare exception. Your child will sense your resolve, or lack of it during the process, and that alone can make a big difference.

Signs of Readiness

Signs of readiness fall into three categories. First comes the physical aspect. Physical readiness starts when your child begins to recognize the urge to go and that he can control the muscles that lets him go. Next comes the willful component which includes telling Mom or Dad when he has the urge, and electing to go on the potty and not in his pants. The third aspect is the learning component which includes how to use the potty, eventually how to wipe himself, pull up his pants, flush the toilet and wash his hands.

Recognizing the Urge

There are a number of ways that toddlers show us that they recognize the urge to go to the bathroom. Some children stand a certain way or hold onto their diaper as they eliminate. It's not unusual for a child to stop what he is doing to concentrate on the process and then come and ask to be changed, or he may find a private place to 'go do his business' and then return to his activity.

Adjusting to the Sensation

Stephanie Taylor, one of our contributing moms writes: "I knew our younger daughter was making the association when she got up out of the bathtub and asked me to put a diaper on her because she had to go pee pee. She knew what her body needed to do and she knew where it needed to be done. Our first challenge was helping her transfer the association from the diaper to the potty chair. Once that was accomplished, we had to help her adjust to the change in the sensation. She was used to urinating with the diaper next to her body and initially she was afraid to release her urine without the presence of a diaper. The sensation was different and she didn't like it. But we made it through the process just fine."

Recognizing Muscle Control

Children do not instinctively understand that they actually control the muscles that hold and release their waste. It can take them a little time to learn this. Once your child has adjusted to the sensation, he needs to understand the muscle control that is involved. After a few successful trips to the potty, it usually begins to click in their minds. A simple statement such as "make the pee-pee come out" may be all that is needed to turn on the light bulb and see wonderful results accompanied by a great, big grin from your toddler. The recognition of bowel control is easier and more natural because children actually have to make some effort to push it out. For most children, the issue is getting them to do that on the potty.

Learning to Use the Muscles

Once a child recognizes the urge, has adjusted to the new sensation and understands that he controls the muscles, it is just a matter of patience and practice. Children need many opportunities to practice so that they can use those muscles at the appropriate time and in the appropriate place.

Telling Mom

After your child learns how to use the potty, the next step is getting him to tell you when he needs to go. This starts with Mom and Dad routinely encouraging the child to sit on the potty. Through repetition he develops the habit of recognizing the urge to go and begins to voluntarily do so on his own. Daytime dryness will usually come first. Once that is well at hand, you will want to work with your child on nighttime dryness.

Where to Begin?

While readiness starts with the child, potty training starts with the parent. Physical development signals when a child is ready, but the timing and the process are the parents' decision. What will potty training look like in your home? What are the general guidelines? What equipment do you need? What approach will you take and what are your timeline goals?

We start our discussion with a few general guidelines for you to consider. Speaking in the affirmative, *do* begin potty training when:

1. You have reviewed and decided which potty training method you will commit yourself to. (The three recommended methods are described on the following pages.)
2. You set time aside to make potty training a priority.
3. When you have both the emotional and training support from your spouse.

Consider postponing potty training if:

1. You sense your child is not physically ready.
2. If you or your child is sick or recovering from an illness or if you are in the early months of pregnancy.
3. If you are about to start or just completed a major house move.
4. If you are in any relational transition such as the passing away of a loved one, or an unresolved family crises.
5. If you are having an extended period of house guests.
6. If it falls squarely in the middle of your family vacation, or holidays.

What Do You Need?

Fortunately, potty training is a relatively inexpensive activity. There are a few things a parent needs, starting with the most expensive item, the potty chair.

The Potty Chair

The most obvious piece of furniture necessary is a potty chair. If you have two bathrooms, say one upstairs and one downstairs, consider having two potty chairs handy. Keep one in the primary bathroom and let the second one be the utility potty chair that gets moved from room to room. Look carefully at the features of the chair before you purchase one. We recommend one that can adapt to fit onto an adult size toilet.

Training Pants

You will also need some training pants, either disposable or traditional cotton. We favor traditional cotton since they have a sponge-like absorbent core. They work well because the child can definitely feel the wetness when he has an accident. Disposable training pants feel too much like his diapers. Diapers can cause the child to regress to the ease of his old pattern of eliminating instead of the new level of effort required to use the potty chair.

Snack Rewards

Since potty training is a skill, goal incentives can be used to reinforce positive behavior. Small treats such as M&M™ type candy, raisins, apple slices, or whatever is appropriate for your child should be in plentiful supply. Rewards will definitely help reinforce positive behavior and a child should be rewarded for staying DRY and get a double reward after using the potty.

Parental Praise and Your Encouragement Team

"Grandma, I went pee-pee in the potty today" announced two-and-a-half year old Bradon upon arriving at Grandma's house for a visit. His instant reward was praise and an extra-large bear hug from his biggest fan. Before you start your training, contact a few significant friends and relatives. Let them know that your toddler is starting the potty training process and ask them to be on the "encouragement team." To hear praise from Mom and Dad is great, there should be plenty of it. But to hear praise from Miss Nancy next door or Aunt Susan over the phone multiplies the excitement of accomplishment.

It also helps the child learn that potty training is not just something important to Mom and Dad but to many people who love him.

Selecting a Method

As stated earlier, the best experts in the field of potty training are the moms who accomplished the task successfully. Remember, potty training readiness starts with the child, but training starts with the parent. How will you approach this skill-oriented task? Take comfort in what other *On Becoming Babywise* mothers discovered. Surveying a significant number of our moms revealed three different strategies, all of which were based on time-line goals that fit Mom's comfort and energy level. The three approaches include:

- *Progressive potty training*—accomplished in one to three days.
- *Casual Progressive potty training*—that spans two weeks to one month.
- *Relaxed-potty training*—that spans four to six months.

All three methods work and represent individual comfort zones for moms. The question is, which one is right for you? Since the potty training itself is a non-moral activity (it is a skill), it has no right or wrong value associated with it. That means, no one method can be deemed right or wrong. And since readiness variables make each family unique, no one method is best all the time. What is best for your child is what is best for you and what is best for you is best for your child. Here is what each method looks like in practice.

Progressive Potty Training

The rational behind the Progressive Potty Training method was first introduced by two psychologists, Nathan H. Azrin and Richard M. Foxx, in the early 1970s. Working with the challenges of mentally handicapped adults, Azrin and Foxx found a sequential approach to helping these people become self-directed in their body elimination. From that research methodology they were able to adopt similar tactics that are now enjoyed by millions of parents. Their book, *Potty Training in Less Than a Day*, is one resource we recommend as a supplement to this section.

There are a number of advantages to this approach. First, it forces moms or dads to focus on the task at hand—potty training and not potty training plus. Second, success is achieved very quickly. If not within hours, certainly within a few days. Third, the child gains an advantage through concentrated practice. When learning any new skill, practice moves all of us to competency. Finally, it helps a child learn bowel-movement control. If you're giving your child plenty of liquids and taking him to the potty frequently to urinate, at some point he will need to have a bowel movement and chances are it will happen during one of these many trips to the potty.

However, while the principles can work for nearly any child, there are a number of reasons why this approach may not be the best for you. First, it takes at least one day (can be as many as three) of complete and uninterrupted attention. This means you must clear your schedule and your home. Siblings go to Grandma's house, the T.V. and radio stay off, and the phone answer machine goes on. Grocery shopping is put on hold for a few days. There is only one thing going on in your house—potty training.

Second, in surveying our *On Becoming Babywise* moms who successfully used the progressive approach, we found a not-so-surprising correlation exists between potty training success and children who complied with parental instructions. Children who obeyed basic instructions, such as "sit down please", "come to Mama", "fold your hands", "do not touch", were completely trained usually within one day, most within two days and all within three days. If your child is not ready instructionally, progressive potty training is probably not the best approach for you or your child. It will create too many unwelcome and unnecessary conflicts.

What You Need to Get Started

This list is similar to the ones offered above but with a slight modification. The snacks and treats needed for the method will serve a dual purpose. First, they are used as a reward but they also serve to increase your child's thirst. Thirst leads to liquid intake which leads to more frequent output.

Snacks

Potato chips, pretzels, sugar coated cereal, candy, ice cream, cookies, carrot sticks, celery and fruit slices can be used. Stay away from anything that is binding. No cheese treats.

Drinks

Mothers tell us they find a wide range of drinks helpful, including juices, Kool Aid™ type drinks, chocolate milk and even soft drinks. The idea here is two-fold. First, the drinks also become a reward reinforcing motivation and second, what goes in must come out. Liquids increase the number of potty training opportunities during the training period.

Equipment

Azrin and Foxx recommend using a doll that wets. You can pick up a gender neutral doll at your local toy store. Some of our moms found using the doll helpful, others discovered they could train their children in a day or so without the doll. Personally, we recommend using the doll as a teaching tool if you can afford it. The purpose of the doll is to walk the child through the entire process from taking a drink to elimination. It is a play-time opportunity in which the child offers water, checks the doll for dryness, and declares that it is time for the doll to sit on the potty. The child sets the doll on the potty and then listens to the doll tinkle in the potty. From there, he or she moves to clean up. This includes dumping the water in the big toilet, pulling up the doll's pants and washing the doll's hands. (This is where hand wipes are handy for little people who cannot reach the bathroom sink.)

How to Get Started

A couple of days before you get started, head for the grocery store with your toddler to specifically pick out all the fun stuff. Tell your toddler that in a couple of days, he can have these drinks and snacks. Make sure they stay out in clear view for the next 48 hours as a reminder. Tie the treats to the upcoming adventure with potty training. If you give in and give him some of the drinks or snacks beforehand, they lose their "fun" value when you really need them. Also, show him the doll and tell him tomorrow he and Mommy are going to play potty training with the doll.

The night before your start date, introduce the doll. Walk the child through each step of the process <u>one</u> <u>time</u>. After the doll goes potty, offer your toddler a small treat for being a "good" teacher and helping the doll learn to use the potty. The purpose of this exercise is to "prime the pump" for tomorrow's activities. At bedtime, make a big deal out of tomorrow morning and what the two of you will do after breakfast. Get Dad and older siblings involved in the pre-encouragement process.

When Tomorrow Comes

When the big day arrives, put training pants on your child and then a loose pair of pants or clothing that comes on and off easily. For girls, this might be a dress. Your fast-track training starts with breakfast and plenty of liquids. Breakfast should be fairly bland. No sugary cereals, syrupy pancakes or cinnamon toast. Save the sweets for later. Right after breakfast start role-playing with the doll.

Your toddler starts by giving the doll a drink. Wait a few minutes and then have him check the doll for dryness. Ask your toddler, "Is your doll dry?" Have him check the doll's pants with his hands. Of course it will be dry, so make sure your toddler praises the doll for staying dry and offer a make-believe reward for the doll's dryness. Wait a few minutes and encourage him to take the doll to the potty. Have him listen to the doll tinkle and clap your hands in praise.

Tinkling is part of the process of staying dry so this is worth a double reward for the doll. You child can help pull off the doll pants, empty the potty, flush the toilet and go play. Once your child walks through the steps a couple of times you then direct your training with him following the same steps. Your toddler will catch on quickly to what is going on because naturally, he wants some treats too. Once you have him checking for dryness, you are halfway to your goal.

The Importance of Timely Rewards

In their book "*Potty Training in Less Than a Day*", Azrin and Foxx touch on critical aspects of timely rewards. Most parents reward only after their child successfully goes on the potty. But your main objective is not getting your child to use the potty but teaching your child to stay dry and clean. Remember Chapter Six and our *how* and *why* discussion? *How* in this case is represented by the use of the potty chair. The *why* is represented by staying dry. Dryness is the greater value. The potty chair is the place a child goes to stay dry and clean. Thus, you do not wait and offer a treat for going potty but rather for staying dry.

Practically what does this look like? You will teach your child how to check himself for dryness. When Mommy asks "Are you dry?" he puts his hands on his pants, and hopefully says "Yes." Capitalize on dryness, this is a big deal. Wait a few minutes and have him sit on the potty. Let him see that you are holding a double treat in your hands. When he tinkles, he gets the double reward and your praise. Maybe it's even time to call Grandma or Miss Nancy next door.

Staying Mindful

Routinely set your timer to remind you to ask the dryness question. Then, instruct him to check and see if he is still dry. Continue to offer your child special beverages throughout the day—lots of them. The more urine output the more he gets use to the new sensation of going without a diaper on.

Stephanie Taylor suggests that in between trips to the bathroom, have your child sit on a folded towel. Just make it his special little seat when he is playing or watching a video or doing some other activity. If he has an accident, the towel will absorb what the training pants and clothing do not. You will find this to be a very helpful, simple safeguard and can eliminate soaking the couch or the carpet.

Potty training for bowel movements usually comes after a child learns to stay dry. There might be some fear associated with passing a stool since this too is a new experience. Make sure that you are giving your child plenty of fruits and vegetables so that their stools are soft enough to pass without difficulty.

The repetition of going frequently helps the child understand what's happening in his body and enables him to see some progress in a very short time. Stephanie Taylor writes, "The biggest obstacle for our children was getting used to the sensation of urinating without a diaper on. Once they got comfortable with that, they quickly began to understand their muscle control. It was exciting to watch them grasp these concepts and see their satisfaction with themselves. After they understand that they control the muscles, it's just a matter of training them to tell you when they need to go. Of course in time, you will move from the potty chair to the 'big' toilet."

For practical reasons, some of our mothers find it helpful to transition their child to the regular toilet soon after they are potty trained. Potty breaks away from home can be a real problem if your child is used to using only the potty chair at home. When you first start this transition, hold the child in place while reassuring him that Mommy or Daddy will not let him fall. With a little practice your toddler will learn very quickly to balance his little bottom on the big toilet.

If the progressive potty training method seems a bit hectic for you, or you cannot clear your calendar completely, consider the *relaxed or casual-progressive* approach.

Relaxed and Casual-Progressive Potty Training

You might wonder when reading the explanation above, "Why would anyone want to stretch the process out if you can get your child trained in hours or days?" Well, there could be a number of good reasons. Kristen shares her story:

"I trained Zachary over a period of four months with good reason. Just when Zachary began to show initial signs of readiness, I found myself expecting our third child. While I did not want to miss this window of opportunity for training, I knew that I did not have the energy to see training through while living with morning sickness. I elected a very relaxed approach to Zachary's training. I had a start date but let Zachary set the end date. We began slowly and gradually. I was not stressed over the fact that he had accidents but encouraged him as they became less and less common. I knew from working with Zachary's older sister that by keeping him on a routine allowed me to work in specific potty breaks. By the time I was feeling better he was both day and night trained."

Karen's story is slightly different. She wrote:

"My husband is a rancher and we have five children. Between crops, livestock and children, our lives are full and our days hectic. Since I do not have the luxury to just drop my kids off at friends or a neighbor, I find it impossible to give undivided attention to the single event of potty training. With five kids, potty training in our home is a family event. All my children were trained within three weeks. I know that some accomplish the task sooner and others slower but a casual, yet progressive style of training fit our family goals and life-style."

Both the *relaxed* and *casual-progressive* approaches to potty training are descriptive in nature not prescriptive. It describes how things actually are, not how someone thinks things ought to be. If you elect one of these two methods, many of the principles listed previously will also be employed. The process though, is stretched over a few weeks or months rather than completed in hours. Here are some general suggestions to get you started with the alternative methods.

First, make certain your family is not in some type of transition or unsettled period of sickness when you begin. If you just moved to a new home or apartment, wait a few weeks until the newness of your move and your daily routine settles in.

Second, once you have a potty chair, have your child sit on it at regular intervals: in the morning, after meals, before and after naps and bedtime. It is important that you do not ask your child if he wants to sit on it. You are the parent. Simply tell him "It's time to sit on the potty."

Third, it is important that you are in a consistent routine when you begin either of these methods. You need to be home for at least two or three days initially to really focus and cement the basic concepts in your child's mind and body even though you are not intending to complete the process in that short of time.

Fourth, make sure you incorporate the reward system mentioned previously. This will direct your toddler's attention to his or her dryness and cleanliness not simply to going potty. Once the child realizes dryness and staying clean is the goal, it is much easier to motivate him to using the potty. Keep the snacks out and available.

Five, be patient. It is a process. Your child will learn day and nighttime control.

General Related Concerns

Potty training, like many aspects of child training, brings up issues you may have never anticipated. As you go through the process, you learn all sorts of little things that no one ever mentioned to you. Here are a few thoughts that will help make the process easier.

Nighttime Dryness

Just as bladder control usually comes before bowel control, daytime dryness usually comes before nighttime dryness. Once your child has mastered daytime dryness, begin working on his nights. Eliminate liquids after 6:00 pm and cut back on giving a drink before bed. Make sure there is a potty stop just before bed.

Bladder Problems

There are two common bladder problems in toddlerhood. One is the child who is constantly having accidents. Often, this is the child who is ignoring the initial urge to go to the bathroom. More on this problem in a moment. The second problem is the child who wants to go to the bathroom too frequently. This child usually is not emptying his bladder completely when he voids. He's in too much of a hurry to get back to his activities so he cuts off the process.

This situation can usually be corrected by encouraging the child to take some extra time at the toilet. Maybe sing a little song or say the ABCs, then take a couple of big breaths and try again to get all the urine out. If the problem continues contact your pediatrician. You want to rule out any possibility of infection or diabetes. But in most instances these problems are behavioral.

Avoiding Messes

Unfortunately potty training messes are some of the most unpleasant. There are some proactive things you can do to reduce the cleanup. For example, when training your son to initially use the potty chair, teach him to lean forward and direct his stream downward into the potty. This will be especially important after you transition him to a regular toilet. Getting him to aim right can prevent a mess.

When he begins to use the "big" toilet, have him sit on the front with his legs straddled, facing the back of the toilet. That gives him a larger target and any spray misdirected hits the bottom of the seat instead of the floor or wall. If you turn him around adult style, you will probably find more urine on the floor than in the toilet.

Don't forget to teach your son, "tap, tap, tap." The penis always has a few drops that never quite make it out. Encourage him to just tap the top of the end of his penis two or three times. This will help get every last drop out.

Instilling Good Habits

From the very first experience sitting on the potty chair, teach your child to wipe properly (girls especially need to be taught to wipe front to back), flush after themselves (or dump the bowl) and wash their hands. Start the way you want to finish. It doesn't matter if you have boys or girls, both should be taught to leave the bathroom neat and clean for those coming after them. As they get older and are able to use the bathroom alone, hold them to the standard of leaving the bathroom in an acceptable manner.

Going Out

Leaving the house when you are potty training can sometimes be a little unnerving. Accidents are a natural part of this process, so you want to be prepared. Take an extra change of clothes or keep extra clothes in the car for emergencies. Some moms use disposable training pants when visiting friends or going to church. As accidents become less frequent, transition out of disposable training pants completely.

Accidents

When accidents happen (and they will), try not to make a big deal out of them. Verbal disappointment may be shown but punishment will not fix it. You will know if it is truly an accident or negligence on the child's part. Some children will have accidents because they refuse to stop playing when they need to go to the bathroom. Some have accidents because they get so excited that they can't pull themselves away from the activity. Under those circumstances, your child should have consequences for their actions or inaction.

Our little friend Peter was completely day and night trained at two. At three years of age he showed a love and aptitude for fun-filled computer games. But with all the excitement this generated, Peter began to have daily accidents. At three years of age, Peter simply could not control both his excitement at the computer and his need to make a bathroom run. The obvious consequence would be to end his computer game. But that did not fix the problem for the next time. The parents eventually removed his privilege of playing computer games for six months. When the privilege was returned, Peter was developmentally ready to do both, enjoy his games and take responsibility for his bathroom needs.

Bowel accidents are actually more controllable then bladder accidents. Most children develop a routine of having a bowel movement at approximately the same time each day (or every other day). When you know your child is due for one, watch for indicators. Taking him to the bathroom and have him sit for a little while usually does the trick.

Bed-wetting

Some children experience bed-wetting or *Enuresis*. The titles refer to children who wet their beds at an age when most children are dry at night. All children are different and just as they grow at different rates, they will achieve nighttime dryness at different rates. Statistics show that by age eight, 90-95% of children who have struggled with bed-wetting are dry at night. By age twelve, only 2-3% of children experience enuresis. (Some children will experience enuresis throughout adolescence.) Bed-wetting is not considered a problem in the medical world until a child is about four or five years old. There could be a variety of causes including the child's inability to waken when the bladder is full.

If you find that your child is having reoccurring nightly accidents, consult your pediatrician. Your doctor can define or rule out any health problems that might be part of the cause. While working with your child, here are some practical things you can try to remedy this problem:

- Encourage your child to wait as long as possible when it's time to urinate. This technique can help to stretch the bladder so it can hold more urine.

- As your child is urinating, have him stop and start a few times. This helps to strengthen the sphincter muscles that hold in the urine.

- Train your child to take responsibility for his wet bedding, but never shame the child because of it. It is not his fault.

- Consider rewarding him for waking up dry, but do not punish him for night accidents.

- Finally, there are bed-wetting alarms that awaken the child as soon as he begins to wet.

- As you move through this process, encourage and support your child while holding him accountable.

Summary

Potty training guidance leads to better and more satisfactory results when a mother has confidence in what she is doing. We wrote this chapter with that goal in mind. It was our desire to provide practical information, offer some workable strategies and wed together plenty of experience to produce a sustained level of confidence in mom and a predictable outcome for your toddler. We are confident that both mom and child will get through this process just fine as a result.

Chapter Eight

Toddler Topic Pool

*I*ssues? We all have them, but toddlers take the prize. When it comes to misunderstood emotions, life-changing breakthroughs and socially unacceptable behavior, your toddler will run away with the trophy screaming, "Mine! Mine!" No toddler necessarily will present you with the same set of struggles as the next, although some areas of concern do tend to connect with others. For example, nap problems could correlate with eating issues, tantrums, and self-control problems.

In our Toddler Topic Pool, we consolidated a number of common topics of interest into one location to better serve your query. Greatly aided by fifteen years of everyday toddler questions this final chapter is both practical and highly relevant to parents of our day. Below is an index of the topics followed by their explanations. For convenience sake, the topic pool is arranged in alphabetical order. Review and become familiar with the list. Toddler parents will typically come back to this resource many times over, sometimes in just one day.

Autism Screening
Biting

Crib to Bed Transitions

Developmental Deprivation

Fears

Frustration Tantrums (see also Temper Tantrums)

Frustration versus Exasperating

Gender Differences

Head-Banging

Mealtime

    Appetite versus Hunger

    Picky Eater

    Mealtime Behaviors

    Snacks

Naps

Parenting Your Child's Emotions

Planned Learning Opportunities

    Roomtime

    Time with Family Members

        • Reading

        • Bathing

        • Walking

        • Touching

    Free Playtime

Positive Speech

Reinforcement Training

Self-Control Training with Hands

Teething

Temper Tantrums (see also Frustration Tantrums)

Thumb-Sucking

Vacation/Traveling

Weaning From Mom or the Bottle

Autism Screening

Autism is an impairing disorder affecting one in every five hundred children. The core defining symptoms include: impaired verbal (speaking) and nonverbal communication, social interactions with other people (physical contact such as hugging or holding), restricted and repetitive behaviors (such as repeating words over and over again) and obsessively following routines. Early detection can lead to early intervention resulting in improved outcome for most young children with Autism. Some early diagnostic indicators include the absence of babbling, pointing or waiving "bye bye" by twelve months of age, absence of even a single word usage by sixteen months and/or no two-word phrases by twenty-four months of age. These indicators do not mean a child is autistic but that further testing is required. Early intervention is important so if you sense something wrong with your young toddler, ask your pediatrician for a neurological referral.

Biting

"I just received another report from his nursery teacher. My Tommy is biting other children and tearing their skin. What is the problem?" Anyone working with children will come across a similar query as above. Child biting is troublesome because it affects more than just the victims. It affects both sets of parents. Parents of the biter are often ashamed and frustrated over their child's aggression. Parents of the victim are often angered by the behavior. To suggest that biting is normal for toddlers is like saying tooth decay is normal. It's normal only because prevention did not take place.

Observation points us to certain constant negative environmental stimulants associated with biters. A noisy environment, inadequate sleep, lack of structure and routine, lack of boundaries in general and over-socialization are but a few. While all of these contribute to aggression in children to some extent, the last is most significant. Biters seem to be part of a group who are prematurely placed in social settings that overwhelm their senses. Clearly they are over-socialized by being placed in too many group activities. Some toddlers simply cannot handle the stress of "too many children around." Group settings include church nurseries, day-care settings, and large birthday parties that may simply overwhelm these children. Biting then becomes a coping skill whenever the child senses encroachment or his own self-serving need is not met.

The only good news about biting is that it is temporary, although it will never be over soon enough for the victims. While biting might diminish, if not dealt with properly and early, the underlying aggression will simply change forms as the child grows. While your immediate solution will be isolation (time-out chairs are not effective), you still need to deal with the underlying problem. When a child bites, use your voice and facial expressions to show that biting is unacceptable. Speak firmly, have the child make eye contact with you while you express your dissatisfaction. The child, of course, needs to be isolated from potential victims, but the real solution is in changing his environment. The child's world must be reduced socially.

At the first sign of biting, try to limit outside activities involving groups of children. This may temporarily include other toddler birthday parties, the church nursery and suspension of any play group activities. When allowing your child to participate in group activities, Mom can volunteer to sit in on the activity and observe her child. This will allow Mom to see what causes him to bite, and Mom can intervene when she realizes he is going to do so. Taking care of the problem in the early toddler phase can eliminate it all together in the preschool phase just around the corner.

Crib to Bed Transitions

The crib-to-bed transition usually occurs between eighteen and twenty-four months of age. A child who is trained to obedience greatly facilitates this transition. It should be obvious that if a parent doesn't require any degree of compliance during the day, then instructions to stay in bed at night or during naps will hold no power. Going from a crib to a bed is a freedom. What will keep the child there? Only one thing, your word. The goal isn't simply to get your child in a bed, but to have the child stay there all night.

To help make the transition smooth for you and exciting for your child, try to include him or her when going out to purchase the new bed. Maybe the child can help Dad set up the bed or shop with Mom to pick out his "big boy" or "big girl" sheets for the bed. Take advantage of the weekend to make the switch. Most dads will be home Saturday morning to help make a big deal out of a child's first night in his or her own bed.

Initially, don't give your child the freedom to get out of bed without your permission. After naps or in the morning, have the child call out to you before getting out of bed. Teach the child a common phrase, such as, "Up, please" or "May I get up, please?" Letting the child have verbal access to you is usually enough to keep him or her in bed.

Finally, when making the transition, buy or build a side rail for the bed. Children move around on the bed during their sleep much more than adults do. Side rails are as much for the parent's peace of mind as for the child's safety. Moving a toddler out of his crib to a bed is a big change for the child and obviously gives the child considerably more freedom. Teaching your toddler to stay in bed is a challenge for many parents.

Developmental Deprivation

The term developmental deprivation does not refer to a child's being deprived of opportunities to learn, but refers to being deprived of the best opportunities to learn. To a large extent, a child's environment has a tremendous influence on learning. We believe learning deprivation occurs when parents consider a toddler's impetuous and momentary desires to be his prime source of learning. For example, allowing a child to walk and move around the house unhindered, without any guidelines, directions, or restrictions, represents a dubious channel of learning. The environment is both too big and overwhelming for a young toddler. Learning is too often accidental and outside the context of the toddler's developing world.

Toddlers need direction and guidance from their parents. They must learn correct, specific responses for specific situations and then be able to transfer the concept learned to other settings. "Do not drop your food" and "Do not touch the stereo," are examples of what we mean. Those actions are different, but the desired response to both is the same—submission to parental instruction. If parents reinforce their instruction in the living room but not in the kitchen, then the child's ability to discriminate between what his parents expect and what they allow becomes clouded.

Fears

Fear is very much part of the human experience. Childhood fears are interwoven with other aspects of development. With the emergence of a child's imaginative abilities, his fears become increasingly concerned with imaginary dangers. Some children have highly active imaginations. Because a child's imagination develops more quickly than his rational side of thinking, he often exaggerates the dangers of any fear-provoking situation. While that might help adults understand what is going on it doesn't take away the reality of fear for the child. The fact is all children are different, all have different experiences and that means some objects and situations are more fear provoking than others. Whether fears are rational or irrational, they are real to your child.

The process by which fear is acquired comes through indirect or intermediate steps. Children learn fear by observing how parents respond to differing situations. Parents may not respond fearfully but may make comments that evoke fear. For example, a Midwestern father generalizing the strength of a thunderstorm, comments to his wife, "The storm is going to blow our house away." While the wife translates Dad's statement to mean there's a big storm coming, their two year old translates it as, "the house will blow away." Thus the child exhibits fear of thunderstorms.

Childhood fears become associated with bad experiences. Fears can originate with visits to the dentist or doctors office, visiting a relative in the hospital or having an unpleasant experience with a dog or cat. Also, fear-provoking thoughts come through television. And while a child may not experience dangers directly, they do so vicariously through the picture tube or inappropriate videos.

In spite of the fact that fears vary from child to child, there is a range of typical fears in early childhood that include: loud noises, large animals, unfamiliar people, dark rooms, high places and the fear of being abandoned. While fear is a natural condition of childhood, there are some things parents can do to help reduce the incidents of fear or compensate for them.

Reducing the incidents results from reducing fearful stimuli. Proactively, a good place to start protecting your toddler from fear-provoking material is limiting his television or video watching. And please do not assume that all children's videos are safe for your toddler, or that they lack fear-provoking material. Even the death of Dumbo's mother can arouse insecurity in a two-year-old. Second, parents can prepare a child for potential fear-provoking stimuli by explaining beforehand what they might see or experience. Do not let your child wander off by himself to pet the horse tied to a hitching post. Pick him up and carry him to the horse, the dog, the goat or whatever.

Prevention will help reduce fear but cuddling is the best medicine in the moment of fear. One of our mothers wrote: "Our daughter, Amy, was terrified of thunderstorms, even as a toddler. When we first heard a storm coming, we learned to not wait until she woke up screaming, as it would take a long time for her to calm down. We went in to get her and would take her downstairs and rock her until the storm passed by, which they do quickly in the Midwest."

Whether it is intervention or calming solutions, nothing can beat the security of Dad or Mom's arms in times of toddler fear.

Children often overcome their fears once they become acquainted with the object of fear. When they discover that the puppy next door is not chasing after them but rather running to play with them, fear takes leave and relief is experienced. In such cases parents must bridge faulty assumptions with reality. Bringing the dog over and playing fetch, thus showing your child that there is nothing to fear will help him overcome his apprehension. The more a child becomes acquainted with a fearful object the sooner he masters his fears by replacing it with accurate knowledge.

A warning of what not to do is appropriate here. Laughing at a child, scolding or criticizing him by calling him names like, "fraidy-cat" or telling the child "you're not afraid" (unless he is really not afraid and this is a controlling technique on the part of the child) is not helpful and works to the child's detriment. When a child is afraid, he has a reason for being afraid even though that reason seems completely unjustified from an adult's perspective. Respect the child's developing sense of fear but also realize that most fears are overcome in the normal process of growth. As a child lives and learns, he tends to view more and more of the unknown from a rational perspective and not a fearful one.

Frustration Tantrums (see also Temper Tantrums)

Frustration tantrums are not the same as temper tantrums. A frustration tantrum happens when a child cannot make his body accomplish the task his mind can clearly understand. For example, when Whitney tried to place her dolls in a circle, one kept toppling over.

She knew in her mind what she wanted to do but could not physically make it happen. Frustration is the basis of these tantrums, not a defiant angry heart. You will naturally desire to help your child when he gets frustrated. You see him in distress and rush to intervene. However, do not be too quick to jump in and fix the problem. You may be encouraging a short temper and a quickness to give up.

Make yourself available but first insist that the child ask for your help. A simple statement such as, "Mom will help you if you want, but you must ask me," puts the burden of cooperative problem solving on the child. This is a virtue to develop in him, because he will need to know how to work with others to solve problems later in life. If you sense a growing frustration and there is no hope of resolving it, then consider playtime over for now and review if the objects of frustration need to be evaluated for age-appropriate play.

Frustration versus Exasperating

There is a difference between exasperating your child and frustrating him. Your toddler will show frustration over many things. He will be frustrated when you ask him to do something he doesn't want to do, when he doesn't get his way, etc. This is normal and to be expected. You exasperate your child when you ask him to do something he is not capable of doing. Parents often over-talk their toddlers, explaining things to them they are not going to understand. A toddler, for example doesn't care if it is cold outside. All the explanations in the world aren't going to convince him of this. If you want him to wear a coat and he is refusing to put it on, simply put it on him yourself.

If you try to teach your toddler to tie his shoes, you will exasperate him. He doesn't have sufficient coordination or the mental problem solving ability to accomplish this. Sometimes we try to advance our children too fast. Frustration then is the child's problem, exasperation is the parent's problem.

Gender Differences

Any grandmother knows that if you put a toy car, ball, stick, doll, blanket and bowl in a room, little boys immediately gravitate toward the car, ball, and stick, while little girls drift to the doll, blanket and bowl. It really doesn't matter where a child is from, whether it be a complex society likes ours or a simple tribal setting in the rain forest. Little boys have a trail of masculine adjectives that distinctly separate them from little girls. Social conditioning? There might be some, but not sufficient enough to alter male and female predisposition embedded in nature's endowment of gender. The fact is, male and female brains are wired differently. Yes, little boys love trucks and little girls love dolls.

We bring this up as encouragement and a warning. Parents should not attempt to gender neutralize their little boys or girls. A delightful example of this was demonstrated by Dr. George Lazarus, MD an associate clinical professor of pediatrics at New York City's Columbia University College of Physicians and Surgeons. He recounted a mother who gave her daughter a bunch of toy trucks only to find her daughter tucking them into bed!

Understanding gender difference helps parents make proper evaluations about their child's progress rather than make speculative evaluations. For example, when a mother says "But his sister was talking at his age", she is making a comparison in language development. But research confirms that girls tend to have a verbal advantage over boys early on. They speak sooner and more comprehensively by three years of age than their male counterparts who arrive at the same level of competency by four-and-a-half years of age.

Yet, boys have other strengths including aptitudes for math skills and completing calculations in their heads sooner then girls. Even the construction of their building blocks demonstrates gender predispositions, or lack of, toward engineering tendencies. Boys are also wired for action. That might be one reason they are always on the go, while their sisters are content to sit and play with their dolls or be entertained in a single location.

Finally, take notice how little boys play together compared to how little girls play. Girls are more relational and will work together to accomplish a common goal. Boys however are far more likely to try and do things "on their own." Of course any wife understands this truth. Just think through the times you may have offered directions to your husband only to hear, "I know where I'm going," as you're headed straight for Siberia.

Head-Banging

The activity of rhythmically banging the head against the wall or side of the crib would naturally alarm most parents. The condition is known as head-banging. An article appearing in the Journal of America Academy of Child Psychiatry (July 1983), describes head-banging as part of normal development in 20 percent of healthy children. Today, research continues to support that conclusion. And while head-banging and body rocking are common in autistic children, these rhythmic motor activities are also normal behaviors in healthy toddlers. Head-banging might appear as early as six months and can continue through the preschool years. It usually takes place at nap or evening sleep time and lasts a few minutes to an hour. Research points out, for unknown reasons that boys are three to four times more likely to be head-bangers than girls.

Alarming as it may be to parents, children usually do not hurt themselves while head-banging. On the contrary theoretical evidence suggests it is actually a form of comfort, not unlike thumb-sucking, stroking a blanket or rocking back and forth. Clinicians agree that although head-banging is an odd way of self-comforting, it is generally harmless and, in most cases, safe to ignore. However, there are some things you can do that might help your child find a better self-soothing mechanism. Some mothers found success in playing soft music when putting the child down to sleep. While no scientific study was conducted on the correlation, some success is always hopeful news.

What you cannot ignore is crib or bed maintenance. The rocking back and forth is more dangerous to the child then the banging of his head, because such motion can loosen the screws and bolts which hold the crib or bed together. Check them periodically.

Mealtime

Mealtime provides a number of challenges and opportunities to teach and learn. This particular category has a number of subdivisions to follow. We begin with appetite versus hunger.

Appetite versus Hunger

"My two-year-old seems hungry all the time, and then when I want him to eat a meal with the family, he's not hungry." Parents in North America have an unjustified phobia that their children are not getting enough food to eat. As a result, mothers (more than fathers), tend to overfeed their children starting when they're babies. In a toddler discussion with a group of moms of one and two-year-olds, it became evident that confusion exists over the difference between appetite versus hunger and eating problems.

Hunger is a biological response triggered by a message sent to the brain when there is a drop in blood-sugar. It is a biological response calling for more fuel. Appetite in contrast is not triggered by blood-sugar but two senses—sight and smell. Appetite has nothing to do with hunger. We eat because something looks goods to us. Or, as I am typing this paragraph my mind is thinking about that piece of pizza left over from last night's dinner. My memory tells me it is something that I would like even though I just had breakfast two hours ago.

Toddlers are the same as adults. Many of their food wants are simply wants, not needs. We are not advising that parents withhold food from a child when hunger is at stake but rather they learn how to monitor real need. Keep your routine, have special snack times, but do not fall prey to giving your child food just because he asks for it. If you error in this, you may end up with the next problem.

Picky Eater

Like all people, your toddler will show preferences in taste. But don't be too quick to say, "Oh, he doesn't like it," then offer something else. While you will occasionally give him what he likes, you must also consider what meets the needs and desires of the entire family. When age-appropriate, offer your child the same foods your family normally eats.

Many finicky eaters are created, not born. As a parent, evaluate your own relationship to food. Are you overly concerned with nutritional intake? Are you yourself a picky eater? Perhaps you are a junk food connoisseur. As hard as it may be, try not to pass on any extreme preoccupation with food. Family mealtime and the kitchen table should not become a war zone; try to make meals a pleasant experience for everyone.

Here are a few points to consider:

- As mentioned above, Americans tend to over-feed their children. Here are some guidelines for serving. One teaspoon per age of child per food. For example, if your toddler is 2-years-old then he should be served 2 teaspoons of peas, 2 teaspoons of rice, 2 teaspoons of applesauce and so on. Have regular times scheduled for meals and stick to them as much as possible. This will help maintain your child's hunger mechanism.

- Avoid giving a child too much to drink. An appropriate amount for a drink is 8 ounces. Sippy cups are often 10-12 ounces. 10 ounces of water given late in the afternoon will cause the stomach to expand to the point that the child is not sufficiently hungry enough at dinner to cooperatively eat foods that are not 'favorites' of the child.

- A child that eats too little and just picks at meals is a child who is probably snacking too much during the day. He is never hungry enough to eat full meals. Set the timer and when it goes off the meal is over. If your toddler hasn't finished his meal a very reasonable logical consequence is the loss of dessert and or the snack for tomorrow.

Snacks

Snacks are fun afternoon breaks, but like anything else, balance is needed. A snack is not a second meal or a substitute for the next meal. How will you know if you're offering too many snacks? Obviously your toddler's eating habits will be affected. He will eat poorly at the next meal or become a picky eater. If you see either happening, cut back on the amount of snacks offered or cut them out altogether. Here are a few helpful hints about snacking:

- You don't have to offer a snack every day.
- Use moderation. Don't let snacks detract from a hearty appetite.
- Don't use food to avoid conflict. It's generally not wise to attempt to influence a child's behavior by offering a snack.
- Do not use food to pacify sad emotions.
- The place for snacking should be consistent—such as in an infant seat or highchair. Avoid allowing your child to crawl or walk around the house or store with a juice drink or snack in his or her hand.
- As a general suggestion, offer snacks in the afternoon, such as right after your child wakes up from a nap.

Naps/Sleep

Sleep is an important part of a child's life and will continue to be a vital aspect of your toddler's day and night. Naps are not an option based on your child's desires. When naptime comes, your toddler must go down. It's that simple. For optimal development, children need daytime rest periods. A toddler's ability to take a nap depends to a large extent on the habits the child has developed in his or her first year. As a general rule, Toddlerwise babies transition to two naps a day at eight months and continue this through sixteen-to-eighteen months. Those naps gradually decrease in length of time from two hours to one-and-a half to one hour. At eighteen to twenty months you transition again to one longer nap in the afternoon usually right after lunch. Here is a list of items to check off relating to naptime:

- Your toddler is ready to drop his morning nap when he is no longer sleeping during that time or when he is taking a long morning nap but not sleeping during his scheduled afternoon nap.
- Move your morning routine 'up' by at least 1/2 hour, including lunch and the scheduled afternoon nap. (If you have additional children, you may keep their routine in place, just adjust it for this particular child.)
- When he is staying fully awake during the morning, meaning that his stamina has returned and he is no longer cranky, etc. then you may move his schedule back down in line with the other children in the family.
- During the transition keep your morning routine as consistent as possible to give his body time to adjust.

g from a single nap to no naps, or from naptime, is discussed in the next book, *On Becoming
Preschoolwise.*

Parenting Your Child's Emotions

"My two-and-a-half-year-old son doesn't like it when I correct his four-year-old brother. He becomes sad because his brother is being taken away for correction and he will lose his playmate. What should I do?" the mother asked. "I'm thinking it might be better if I didn't correct my four-year-old if it makes my two-year-old sad."

Every child enters life with the propensities for both pleasant and unpleasant emotions. Most parents realize this truth and consequently attempt to find ways to make childhood a happy time for their offspring. Parents recognize that a happy child is a pleasure to be with, easier to teach, exhibits longer sustained periods of self-control and self-entertainment. But is happiness really the ultimate goal of parenting?

One of the greatest mistakes a parent can make however is attempting to parent a child's emotions and not the child. Please note this distinction. We are not saying a child's emotions are not important, but rather attempting to parent the single category of emotions is not the same thing as attempting to parent the whole child. Every child will experience both pleasant and unpleasant emotions. Hopefully, your child will know much more of the first than the second.

The experience of positive emotions, like joy, happiness, affection, esteem and the sense of discovery leads to feelings of security and confidence. This in turn helps the child face and properly react to the negative emotions of worry, jealousy, envy, fear, disappointment, anxiety, and frustration. But parenting to create all the right emotions and avoid all the negative emotions is both unwise and unhealthy. Such an approach holds the parents hostage. Everything is guess-work.

When you attempt to create all the right feelings you abandon other significant values necessary to raise a well-adjusted child. In our opening example, the mom was willing to put aside her four-year-old's wrong behavior to satisfy the happiness of her two-year-old. She was willing to suspend a life needed lesson in virtuous self-control, a tool of life, for a momentary state of happiness.

If happiness is the highest value to offer children, then other "good" values such as honesty, compassion, self-control, self-entertainment, obedience, submission, and patience are all subservient. If there is a context that pits virtues with the emotion of happiness, then happiness must dominate. But the developmental fallout with this approach are numerous. The child that is pampered or shielded from unpleasant experiences is ill-prepared to meet the disappointments, frustration, and other unpleasant experiences that life brings. Parenting a single emotion or a range of common emotions is a poor substitute for parenting the whole child—his heart, his head and body, and emotions.

Planned Learning Opportunities

Learning opportunities should be predominantly the result of planning, not chance. The establishment of healthy learning patterns is the result of providing the right learning environment, one in which controlled stimuli (those factors that normally call for curiosity and investigation) becomes part of your toddler's day. To achieve this end, plan some structured time into his waketime. Those opportunities will include: 1) structured playtime and roomtime alone, 2) time with family members and 3) free playtime. (See Chapter Four on "Structuring Your Toddler's Day".)

Roomtime

We maintain that play serves the learning process. But the spontaneous interest of toddlers is not the only influence on their play, since parents control to a large extent the environment in which they learn. For this reason, both structured and nonstructured learning environments are needed. Structured playtime is a specific time during the day when a child has time to play by himself or herself. It starts in the early months with the playpen and advances to roomtime.

Around eighteen to twenty-months of age, you can begin to see if your toddler is ready for roomtime. The principles of roomtime are the same as for the playpen, but you will be using the child's room as his or her play area. Playing in his own room doesn't mean the child can do whatever he pleases. The child shouldn't be allowed to ransack the room, take out all available toys or rearrange the furniture. Some supervision is necessary. Initially, a gate may be required, but your goal is to have your child play alone in the room for an extended period of time without any physical restrictions. As the child develops self-control and demonstrates responsible behavior, you can award the child freedoms.

There may be occasions when roomtime actually will be located somewhere other than in a child's bedroom, such as when the child shares a bedroom with one or more siblings and that situation makes having a consistent roomtime period in that location unpractical.

Roomtime is simply playpen time with extended boundaries, so roomtime can be located somewhere else in the house—in a corner of the kitchen, for example. It's important to increase a child's boundaries as the child develops.

Many parents confuse roomtime with free playtime (to be discussed in a moment). Roomtime is assigned to the child. It's a time determined by Mom, not the child. Mothers sometimes say to us, "My son plays in his room on his own." That's nice, but will he play in his room in response to Mom's instruction? Usually the answer is "No". Just because a child voluntarily plays in his room doesn't mean he is having "roomtime", as we are using the term. It's one thing for a child to do what he wants when he wants to; it's another thing for him to follow a parent's direction.

Yielding to parental instruction as standard behavior is part of the learning structure you're attempting to establish. The self-control inherent in obedience is the same self-control that advances the child in other disciplines.

Time with Family Members

There are some obvious activities which take place during waketime that include interaction with one or more family members. It's important to enjoy your relationship with your toddler, but you must find the right balance between playing with your child and becoming your child's sole source of entertainment.

There is no "right" amount of time that must be devoted to family play activities. But if you find that your child clings to you, refuses to go to Dad or siblings or cries when you leave the room, it may be the result of too much playtime with Mom. In this case, the child is overly dependent on the mother for entertainment and is comfortable only with her. Such a situation closes off opportunities for others to participate in the child's life. Here are some safe play activities in which all family members can participate:

- Reading. It's never too soon to read to your child or to show colorful picture books (especially cardboard or plastic ones that he or she can explore alone). Many children enjoy being read to long before they can understand the words. The continuous flow of sound, the changes in vocal inflections and facial expressions attract a child's attention. Nestling your child in your lap when you read further enhances this experience.
- Bathing. This is another activity of your toddler's day when interaction takes place. You can sing to your child, tell him or her which part of the body you are washing or just have fun splashing. However, you should make sure the splashing doesn't get out of hand. Remember, balance is the key concept in the training process. We recommend you bathe your toddler and not bathe with him or her. A child might have several bath props, such as plastic toys, a cup or a spoon that make bathing a fun time.
- Walking. Taking time for a stroll outside is a great activity for the two of you. By the time your toddler is walking, he is also curious about the big world outside his house. A regular walk becomes a big adventure for your toddler and it is healthy for you, too.
- Touching. A healthy influence on a child's emotional development is the type of physical touching that comes through

play activities. Play is an important part of a child's growth. Touch communicates intimacy, and together, touch and play form a winning combination. Lying down on the couch, floor or bed and blowing kisses, tickling and physically playing with your toddler are necessary components for healthy relationship formation.

Free Playtime

"Free playtime" isn't a time when you allow your toddler to cruise the house looking for entertainment. Rather, it refers to planned and impromptu times when a toddler plays with his or her toys at a play center. A play-center is a small, safe area containing a basket or box of age-appropriate toys that the child can go to at will. Parents can set up play-centers in the kitchen, bedroom, living room, or any convenient spot that will allow them to observe the child from a distance. Keep the majority of toys at the play-center. That doesn't mean if the play-center is in the kitchen there should be no toys in the child's bedroom. It does mean however, that toys are not left in every corner of the house for the child's convenience.

Play is important to a child. The repetition of play activities gives a child a chance to develop and consolidate the skills that a particular kind of play requires. It also affords the child an opportunity to resolve mechanical problems with his or her toys. Another parent-directed skill is cleanup. When play is over, help your child with this task without trying to do it all for him or her. Say to your child, "Playtime is over; let's clean up. Mommy will help," or, "Let's put your toys in your play box." By directing the child to put some, if not all of the toys back, you are defining the parameters of playtime. Those parameters include the concept that playtime is not over until all the toys are picked up. That process instills a sense of order. It also impresses on the child a sense of personal responsibility, something every society needs in order to survive.

In the early toddler months, keep the toys simple. Stacking blocks, balls, objects that can be manipulated with the hands and colorful books are but a few examples. Play is important, and free playtime is as important as structured playpen time and roomtime. Enjoy your child and let him or her enjoy exploring the world through play.

The type of behavioral adjustments a child makes in life are greatly influenced by the child's understanding of his or her environment, other people and awareness of self. Waketime serves growth and development. But waketime activities must be organized, rather than being free-for-all experiences which fall between meals and naps. When a child receives guidance in establishing right patterns of behavior, learning is advanced.

Positive Speech

Toddlers are spirited little beings, always on the go. They give us plenty of reason to keep our guard up and as a result we spend as much time restraining wrong behavior as we do encouraging right behavior. While words of restraint are necessary throughout the training process, we must attempt to also communicate with positive words, especially during the toddler phase where the foundation of language is cemented. This will take self-discipline, but the efforts will pay great dividends.

When communicating with your children, attempt to speak as often as possible in the positive not the negative. If there is something you don't want your child to do, then communicate your desire for restraint by speaking in favor of what you want done. Or we can say it this way. As often as possible use the negative of the virtue not the negative of the vice. Did you get all that? Surely if any concept needs explaining this one does. Most "wrong" behavior is broken into the vice or virtue category. The vice category is negative, the virtue is positive. If a child does something wrong parents tend to describe the negative side of the vice. For example, a parent will comment to their two-year-old, "Hitting your sister was foolish". Foolish represents the negative of the vice. When you use the negative of the positive, you would say, "Hitting your sister was unkind". Unkind is the negative side of the virtue. Instead of saying, "You're lying" (the negative side of the vice), consider, "You're not telling Mommy the truth". Instead of saying, "You're acting selfish", consider, "You're not thinking of others". Using the negative side of the virtue is far better than using the negative side of the vice when describing a child's naughty behavior.

You can use positive speech in other ways. Here are a few more examples. Instead of saying, "Don't spill your cereal on your way to the table," consider saying, "See how carefully you can carry your cereal to the table." Instead of saying, "Don't get out of bed," consider, "Obey Mommy and stay in bed." Instead of saying, "Don't talk so much," consider, "You need to learn to become a better listener." Instead of saying, "Don't leave a mess for everyone else to clean up," consider, "Be responsible and clean up after yourself."

With toddlers there will always be plenty of justifiable "don'ts." "Don't touch the knives." "Don't play with the stereo." "Don't hit the dog." Such prohibitions are appropriate with young children. But as they mature, they need positive direction. Consider the transfer from negative to positive speech a good habit to get into.

Reinforcement Training

Generally, there is a purpose behind a child's actions. To achieve his purpose, the child may use methods that help him and drop those which do not. Any behavior that is supported by parents is called reinforcement training; behavior which is discouraged by them is called non-reinforcement training. Both good and bad behavior are subject to reinforcement training. If parents give in to whining for example, they reinforce it. If they take immediate steps to correct and prevent the whining, they discourage it. If parents praise a child for self-generated initiative, such as making his bed in the morning without being told, they further encourage the behavior. When parents do not give praise, they discourage the behavior. Parents need to be cognitive of the benefits and liabilities of reinforcement training. Positive behavior should be encouraged; negative behavior must be discouraged.

Self-Control Training with Hands

Do you have one? You know: a mover and a shaker, a high energy, perpetual motion, chase-his-own-tail kid. How many times have you tried to slow your little missile? "Calm down." "Settle down." "Sit still." "Stop moving." "Stop kicking." "Put your hands down." "Sit on your hands." "Be still for a moment." Has it ever worked for longer than a millisecond? Have you ever thought about what "settle down" or "slow down" looks like to a three-year-old? These are abstract concepts, metaphors. A three-year-old doesn't have a clue what you mean.

The call came in a moment of desperation. "Jessie, I'm getting a little apprehensive about our breakfast meeting with the Ezzos this Saturday. My two little ones do not do well sitting for long periods of time. Help!" "Louise," Jessie said, "there is a nifty little thing that helps children gain self-control in moments when you most want it and they most need it. Are you ready?" "Yes!"

"When you begin to see those early signs that your kids are going to lose it, physically or verbally, instruct them to fold their hands and work on getting some self-control." Louise began the training immediately. She and her family did meet the Ezzos that Saturday for breakfast. Toward the end of the meal, a wandering little leg popped itself up on sister's chair. That would normally be enough of a catalyst to energize the two-and-a-half-year-old and a four-year-old into all-out playtime, right there in the restaurant—but Mom had another plan.

Instead of all the classic begs, bribes and threats, she simply said: "Girls, we're not quite ready to go yet. I want you to fold your hands and get some self-control."

Would you believe those two little girls sat still, with their hands folded in their laps? In less than a minute, they had subdued their impulsive behavior without a war of words with Mom. Afterwards, Mom pulled out some crayons and let them color on the paper napkins.

Teach your child that self-control begins with the folding of her hands. That is a wonderful concrete way for her to understand calmness. Children as young as eighteen-months can learn this wonderful skill. How does it work? Because a child's body is full of energy, the energy must go somewhere. When Mom says, "Settle down" or "Sit still" or "Stop kicking," nothing happens because she did not redirect the energy. When Mom says, "Honey, I want you to fold your hands and get some self-control," now the energy is directed right to those folded hands. Yes, it is that simple.

Have you ever experienced a verbal war in the backseat during a drive to Grandma's house? Try this: "Kids, neither one of you is speaking kindly. For a few minutes we are not going to talk. I want you to fold your hands and get some verbal self-control." (Don't forget to get a "Yes, Mom.") Why does it work? Verbal energy needs to go somewhere, too. It goes to the hands. How about a two-year-old throwing a fit in his booster chair because his food is not coming fast enough? Try having him fold his hands and look at them. This nifty trick also helps facilitate patience.

Parents should always try to help a child gain self-control before the child crosses the bridge of trouble, not afterward. The hand-folding exercise does exactly that. It is a wonderful tool that can be used at checkout counters, school functions, swim lines, dentist's offices or during that longer-than-usual sermon.

Hand-folding handles all the excessive body energy that makes self-control so difficult. After all, if you want your child to settle down, that energy has to go somewhere. Now, instead of it going into squabbling or cartwheeling or whispering, it can go into the hands.

Another amazing thing about hand-folding is how quickly it brings about self-control. Usually only thirty to ninety seconds need to elapse before Mom can say, "Okay kids, you can let go of your hands." Your child only needs to fold her hands long enough to gain self-control in the moment. Once that is accomplished, Mom can redirect the child's energy to productive activities (like coloring on paper napkins).

It is important to teach this technique when things are calm. If you're already in the conflict, your children are not going to be especially attentive or receptive pupils. You may have your child practice this at the table while you finish up last-minute mealtime preparations. Make it a fun game in the beginning. Demonstrate how to achieve self-control in a peaceful time, so that when things begin to get out of hand, you've got the cure in place.

This simple technique will become second nature to your child and will work wonders in creating the peace your family deserves.

Teething

Often children who have been characterized by sleeping through the night might start waking up in the middle of the night around 20 months. Please know that a toddler's 'two-year molars' might be coming in, and this can be a long process. You can try rubbing Orajel™ on his gums and giving him Tylenol™ to help with the pain. If your toddler has been waking up for a few nights in a row and you have determined he is teething, you can give him Tylenol™ before you go to bed so that it is working at it's peak during your toddler's active sleep cycle, which is when he is waking up crying.

Temper Tantrums (see also Frustration Tantrums)

Parents cannot expect that a child will achieve maturity in emotional behavior any sooner than he will achieve maturity in other areas of development. How he controls and expresses his emotions is far more important than the fact that he merely controls or expresses himself. The first is a learned state, the second is the natural state.

There are right ways to express feelings and wrong ways. Throwing temper tantrums is the wrong way.

The propensity for throwing temper tantrums is a normal phase of development. That is not to say temper tantrums must be allowed. Tantrums are triggered by disappointment and frustration. A temper tantrum, whether thrown by a child or an adult, is a coping mechanism occurring because an individual has not learned how to correctly manage disappointment. As future control over this emotion increases, the potential for tantrums decreases. Meanwhile, you still need to deal with it. Here are some suggestions:

1. Take note of when and where your child throws his fits. Is it only in public, just before or after a meal or when he is tired and in need of a nap? If a pattern exists, knowing it will help you prevent tantrums before they happen.
2. As difficult as it may be, try not to talk a child out of his tantrum. Without realizing it, you are encouraging the behavior by rewarding it with attention and gentle words. To work effectively, a tantrum needs a sympathetic audience. Talking provides that audience. Speaking beseechingly to a child in a tantrum is like granting a terrorist's demands.
3. Use isolation for temper tantrums. Deposit the child in his room or on the couch until he settles down. That may take ten minutes or longer.
4. One technique that some have found helpful in such cases is to physically hold the child. Sit down and hold that child until you feel the struggling arms and flailing legs surrender to your will. Don't let go. When he surrenders, the tantrum is over. And you will see a more peaceful child.

5. Do not add the question "Okay?" to the end of your instructions. "Johnny, we're going to leave the store now, okay?" This is begging for trouble. What if it is not okay with Johnny? Try it this way: "Johnny, we're going to be leaving the store soon. I want to hear a 'Yes, Mommy.'" A child will not say "Yes, Mommy," and then throw a tantrum.

6. Teach delayed gratification. This must become a reality in your child's life. He simply cannot have everything he wants when he wants it. Immediate gratification training only heightens a child's anxiety when the pattern is not maintained.

Thumb-Sucking

It is best to stop thumb-sucking before age two when possible. We are advocates of a gradual process that includes the use of substitution instead of suppression. For example, you can start by limiting your toddler's thumb-sucking during the day, allowing it during naptime and bedtime only. When you see your toddler put her thumb in her mouth, gently remind her to remove it. You might give her something to do with her hands during this time. Most children suck their thumbs to soothe themselves, so again, give them a soft blanket or stuffed animal to hold instead.

Vacation/Traveling

"My husband and I will be traveling for the next couple of weeks with our toddler son. How do we maintain his routine, especially when we move through other time zones?" This is one of the most common questions received in our office. There are two considerations to focus on when traveling: 1) training your toddler to sleep other places than in his crib, and 2) adjusting your toddler's routine to each new time zone.

In preparation for travel, begin a few weeks in advance putting your child down for his naps or nighttime sleep in the playpen. For a couple of nights, put the playpen in the living room, family room or your bedroom. Drape the outside of the playpen on two sides with towels or extra toddler blankets, then take those blankets or towels along on your trip; or borrow some towels when you arrive at your destination. The blankets or towels serve to enclose the child's sleep environment and reduce potential distractions. If your child pulls the towels into the playpen, then stop using them. You want to avoid a situation that could endanger his health or safety.

If your trip is to an adjacent time zone, time adjustments will be fairly automatic. However, when flying through three or four time zones, make the adjustments to your toddler's routine once you arrive. The type of adjustment depends on whether you are traveling east to west or west to east. With the first, you have an extended day; with the second, you have an early night. If you have an extended day, add another feeding and possibly a catnap. If you go east, split the bedtime difference in half between the old and new time zones. For example, your toddler's 7:00 p.m. West Coast bedtime is equivalent to 10:00 p.m. East Coast time. Splitting the difference between the two time zones would make your toddler's first East Coast bedtime 8:30 p.m. Over the next couple of days, work his bedtime back to 7:00 p.m., making as many adjustments as needed to his daytime routine.

We suggest you limit sweet drinks and snacks while traveling. A long trip is a particularly bad time to add extra sugar to your toddler's diet, and extra snacks can suppress hunger to the point where it can affect behavior. Disrupting your toddler's routine can affect his sleep/wake cycles, something neither you or your toddler want to have happen while traveling.

Carla Link, our contributor to Chapter Five adds some practical insights. She starts with this warning: There are three things that in combination lead to an out-of-control toddler. They are; too much sugar and pop, too little sleep and too many freedoms. Avoid these three.

Wise parents will plan the best way to manage their toddlers while on vacation. The following are some of her suggestions.

1. Looking at the entire vacation, determine how to get naps in for your toddler. If it is not possible on a particular day for your child to have a nap, then try to see that he gets to bed earlier than his normal bedtime on that particular night. Over-tired toddlers are difficult to deal with and can easily make vacation a memorable trip for all the wrong reasons! Try to plan your activities so that your toddler gets to bed at his normal time every other day.

2. If you are staying with relatives and want to go out at night, ask them if they know of teens who will toddlersit for you.

3. Try to avoid a steady diet of fast-food. Prepare sandwiches in advance—keep these and fresh fruit and juice in a cooler. If you are going to frequently use hotels, consider purchasing a cooler that serves as a refrigerator (available at truck stops) and can be plugged into a cigarette lighter in a vehicle and with a converter into a wall socket in a hotel room. Your toddler will behave much better if you avoid giving him pop to drink and fast food and pizza as a steady diet.

4. Do take a Pak-and-Play (playpen) along if your toddler has not yet transitioned into a bed.

5. If you are driving on a long-trip with your toddler, figure out how many hours you will be in the car each day. Plan activities for your toddler using the same schedule you use at home, working in 15 minute to 1/2 hour segments. Rotating toys will keep him occupied for longer periods of time. Many vehicles have some sort of television. Do use videos, but keep in mind the attention span of a toddler, keep them to 30 minutes and rotate them with other activities.

6. Do stop often for potty breaks at rest stops and let your toddler run on the grass/picnic area. Give him an inflatable ball to chase around.

7. If you are flying, make sure you take advantage of the opportunity to pre-board. Determine the amount of time you will be traveling, including time sitting between flights, if applicable. Again, using the routine you have at home, rotate activities for your toddler. If you have a long wait between flights, take your toddler for a walk. Don't use a stroller as your child needs to work off some energy before he is expected to sit on a plane.

8. Check with your airline regarding food options. This seems to change frequently with most airlines. And remember, airlines now are starting to sell their lunches rather than provide them for free, so pack food and drink for your toddler and yourself. And do not forget to take his favorite stuffed animal and blanket on the plane.

9. Whenever traveling, whether by car, train, or plane—do take a stroller. If you are limited by weight restrictions, consider purchasing an inexpensive 'umbrella' type stroller for the trip. There

will be times your toddler will be too heavy for you to carry. He can't be expected when sight-seeing to 'keep up' with those with longer legs.

10. Do realize when you are vacationing in the summer that long periods of time in the sun and heat will wear your toddler down and make him crankier than usual. If you are vacationing on the beach consider getting a large beach umbrella and have him sit under it for periods of time during the day. This can be used for blanket time.

Weaning Your Toddler

Weaning, by today's definition, is the process by which parents offer food supplements in place of, or in addition to, mother's milk. That process begins the moment parents give their toddler formula or when the child first tastes cereal. From that moment on, weaning occurs gradually.

From the Breast

The duration of breast-feeding has varied in the extreme from birth to fifteen years. No one can say for sure what age is ideal. For some it may be six months, for others a year. Breast-feeding for more than a year is a matter of preference, since adequate alternatives to breast milk are usually available. At birth, infants depend totally on their caregivers to meet their physical needs. But they must gradually move toward independence, one small step at a time. One such step for your toddler is the ability to feed himself or herself. You can start by eliminating one nursing period at a time, going three to four days before dropping the next one. That time frame allows a mom's body to make the proper reductions in milk production.

Usually the late-afternoon feeding is the easiest to drop first, since it is a busy time of day. Replace each feeding with six to eight ounces of formula or milk (depending on the child's age).

From the Bottle

At a year most infants can begin transitioning from a bottle to a cup. Although young toddlers can become very attached to the bottle, you can minimize that problem by not letting the toddler hold the bottle for extended periods of time. There is a difference between drinking from a bottle and playing with it. Weaning takes time, so be patient. Begin by eliminating the bottle at one meal, then at another, and so on.

The Next Step

It seem like it happens over night. Suddenly your one-year-old is blowing out candles on his second birthday. From his first steps of exploration to potty training success the factors of growth and development dominated the first twenty-four months of your toddler's life. But it doesn't stop there. What are the next developmental transitions to take place?

On Becoming Preschoolwise picks up where this book leaves off. The changes over the next two-and-a-half years are nothing short of amazing. Between two and four years of age, your toddler becomes a little boy or little girl. Gender differences begin to dominate. He is not just walking but running. He is no longer driven by simple curiosity but discovers a whole new world of imagination. His mind is ready to advance to the next level of cognitive activity. He moves away from his own sense of self-play and joins in group play. Friends begin to matter more, internal controls awaken the child's sense of others, and his brain and heart both compete for attention. Are you ready to parent a preschooler?

We'll be ready when you are. *On Becoming Preschoolwise* takes you and your toddler to the next level of physical, intellectual and social advancement. You will learn about the best way to nurture your child's developing brain, conscience, sense of play, social world, self, and relationship with friends and family. We address school readiness with two chapters devoted to educational readiness and laying the foundation for kindergarten even though it is a few years away. What must your child be able to do the first day of school and how will you prepare him for intellectual and social challenges? We provide a list of recommended toys and educational aids to help prepare your child's mind to compete in a world of ideas. And of course, we offer age-old and practical advice on correction and encouragement. It's all there for you. *On Becoming Preschoolwise*, the next step in your parenting journey.

Index